Contents

Essanaye's Sesame Beef Stir Fry 5
Okinawan-Style Pad Thai 6
Monica's Japanese Garlic Dollop Shrimp 7
Curry Tofu Stir-Fry 8
Bekki's Mexican Egg Rolls 9
Spicy Green Beans and Pork, Asian Style 10
Chinese Braised Zucchini 11
Easy Japanese-Style Vegan Collard Greens 12
Apple Fried Rice 12
Pad Thai with Spaghetti Squash 14
Pineapple Fried Rice with Ham 15
Muscat Gosht (Lamb in Spicy Tomato Gravy) 15
Vegetarian, Tofu-Less Stir-Fry 16
Kristy's Le Tofu Orange 17
Summer Special Shrimp and Fruit Fried Rice 18
Balsamic Vinegar and Ginger Bok Choy 19
Honey-Ginger Shrimp and Vegetables 20
Shrimp Lo Mein with Broccoli 21
'Chinese Buffet' Green Beans 22
Super Easy Stir-Fried Cabbage 22
Zucchini Noodles Pad Thai 23
Authentic Pad Thai Noodles 24
Chicken and Snow Peas 26
Pork and Bamboo Shoots 26
Chicken Afritada (Filipino Stew) 27
Stir-Fried Mushrooms with Baby Corn 28
Bitter Melon and Black Bean Sauce Beef 29
Pork, Apple, and Ginger Stir-Fry with Hoisin Sauce 30
Grapes and Rice Stir Fry 31
Spicy Beef Filet in Oyster Sauce 32
Breakfast Fried Brown Rice 33

- Stir-Fried Tofu with Cashews 34
- Mild Thai Beef with a Tangerine Sauce 35
- Easy Vegan Red Curry with Tofu and Vegetables 36
- Batagor Bandung (Indonesian Fried Tofu) 37
- Fried Rice with Lychees (Koa Pad Lin Gee) 38
- Chinese Dong'an Chicken 39
- Easy Chicken and Vegetable Stir-Fry 40
- Bok Choy with Pine Nuts and Sesame Seeds 41
- Chicken, Snow Pea, and Cashew Fried Rice 41
- Garlic-Mushroom Chicken Thigh Stir-Fry 42
- Fried Rice with Corned Beef, Spinach, and Eggs 43
- Paleo Spicy Shrimp Stir-Fry 44
- Corned Beef Fried Rice with Mint 44
- Thai Pad Thai Noodles 45
- Panang Curry with Chicken 46
- Thai Spicy Basil Chicken Fried Rice 47
- Easy Pineapple Chicken 48
- Myra's Basil Chicken Stir Fry 49
- Crispy Shrimp Tempura 50
- Beef Lo Mein 51
- Mushroom Pepper Steak 52
- Pineapple Fried Rice II 52
- Caribbean Jerk Stir-Fry 53
- Erika's Ginger Beef 54
- Super Simple Spicy Fried Tofu 55
- Green Curry with Sweet Potato and Aubergine (Eggplant) 56
- China Sun Chicken 57
- Makato's Bacon Fried Rice 58
- Spicy Ma Po Tofu 58
- Ultimate Pad Thai 59
- Spence's Secret Thai Red Shrimp Curry 61
- Wat Wah Tat 62
- Fettuccine Bombay 63

Vegetarian Thai Fried Rice (Khao Pad Je)	64
Japanese Spicy Spare Ribs	65
Easy-Peezy Caramel Granola	66
Nicola's Pad Thai	66
Almond Vegetable Stir-Fry	68
Asian Pork Linguine	69
Vegetable Pad Thai	70
Peanut Chicken Stir-Fry	70
Thai Beef Stir-Fry	71
Sirloin Stir-Fry with Ramen Noodles	72
Sweet-and-Sour Beef	73
Simple Shrimp Pad Thai	74
Turkey Asparagus Stir-Fry	74
Colorful Shrimp Pad Thai	75
Saucy Thai Beef Noodles	76
Goong Tod Kratiem Prik Thai (Prawns Fried with Garlic and White Pepper)	77
Tsao Mi Fun (Taiwanese Fried Rice Noodles)	78
Fiery Chicken Thigh Stir-Fry	79
Cashew Chicken with Water Chestnuts	80
Crispy Ginger Beef	81
Super-Simple, Super-Spicy Mongolian Beef	82
Caramelized Pork Belly (Thit Kho)	83
Moo Goo Gai Pan	84
Orange Peel Beef	85
Cashew Chicken Stir Fry	86
Pad Thai Quinoa Bowl	87
Healthier Pan-Fried Honey-Sesame Chicken	88
Chinese Take-Out Shrimp with Garlic	89
Pork Tofu with Watercress and Bean Sprouts	90
Dol Sot Bi Bim Bap	91
Sesame Pepper Stir Fry	93
Charred and Herbed Corn Salad with Crab	94
Pad Thai with Tofu	94

Sichuan Pork Stir-Fry ... 96
Singapore Beef Stir-Fry ... 97
Chicken Singapore Noodles ... 98
Snappy Chicken Stir-Fry ... 99
Asparagus Turkey Stir-Fry ... 100
Coconut Curry Shrimp ... 100
Thai Shrimp Stir-Fry ... 101
Mandarin Pork Stir-Fry ... 102
Asparagus Tofu Stir-Fry ... 102
Spicy Chicken Lettuce Wraps ... 103
Thai-Style Brisket ... 104
Pork 'n' Pea Pod Stir-Fry ... 105
Balsamic Pork Stir-Fry ... 106
Stir-Fried Scallops and Asparagus ... 107
Mexican Fiesta Steak Stir-Fry ... 107
Sugar Snap Pea Stir-Fry ... 108
Beef Orange Stir-Fry ... 109
Sizzling Chicken Lo Mein ... 109
Chicken Soba Noodle Toss ... 110
Peking Shrimp ... 111
Orange Beef and Asparagus Stir-fry ... 111
Curried Fried Rice with Pineapple ... 112
Ginger-Peach Pork Skillet ... 113
Nutty Chicken Stir-Fry ... 114
Chicken Chow Mein ... 114
Shrimp Lo Mein ... 115
Shrimp and Broccoli Stir-Fry ... 116
Pork and Vegetable Stir-Fry with Cashew Rice ... 117
Sweet-Spicy Chicken and Vegetable Stir-Fry ... 118

Essanaye's Sesame Beef Stir Fry

Prep: 25 mins **Cook:** 15 mins **Additional:** 8 hrs **Total:** 8 hrs 40 mins **Servings:** 6 **Yield:** 6 servings

Ingredients

- ½ cup soy sauce
- ½ cup white sugar
- ⅓ cup rice wine vinegar
- ⅓ cup minced garlic
- 1 tablespoon sesame seeds
- 1 pound round steak, thinly sliced
- ¼ cup peanut oil
- 2 cups 1-inch sliced asparagus
- 1 cup sliced fresh mushrooms, or more to taste
- 1 sweet onion, chopped
- 1 red bell pepper, sliced
- 1 bunch green onions, chopped into 1-inch pieces
- 1 cup whole cashews
- 1 tablespoon sesame seeds
- 1 tablespoon cornstarch
- 1 tablespoon water
- 1 tablespoon sesame seeds

Directions

- **Step 1**

  Whisk soy sauce, sugar, rice wine vinegar, garlic, and 1 tablespoon sesame seeds in a bowl; pour into a resealable plastic bag. Add beef, coat with marinade, squeeze out excess air, and seal bag. Marinate beef in the refrigerator overnight.

- **Step 2**

  Heat peanut oil in a wok or large skillet over medium-high heat; cook and stir beef and marinade until beef is well-browned, about 5 minutes. Stir in asparagus, mushrooms, onion, bell pepper, and green onions; cook and stir until vegetables begin to soften, 3 to 4 minutes. Add cashews and 1 tablespoon sesame seeds; continue cooking until vegetables are tender, 2 to 3 minutes more.

- **Step 3**

  Mix cornstarch and water in a small bowl; stir into beef stir fry until sauce is thickened, about 3 minutes. Sprinkle with remaining 1 tablespoon sesame seeds.

Cook's Note:

If you don't plan on consuming the entire batch the first meal, I suggest you omit the cashews altogether, or add them to each plate when served. They will turn soggy and not be very appealing the second day.

Nutrition Facts
Per Serving:

476.3 calories; protein 23.7g 47% DV; carbohydrates 38.3g 12% DV; fat 27.2g 42% DV; cholesterol 40.2mg 13% DV; sodium 1379.8mg 55% DV.

Okinawan-Style Pad Thai

Prep: 10 mins **Cook:** 20 mins **Additional:** 10 mins **Total:** 40 mins **Servings:** 8 **Yield:** 8 servings

Ingredients

- ½ cup rice wine vinegar
- ½ cup white sugar
- ¼ cup oyster sauce
- 2 tablespoons tamarind pulp
- 1 (12 ounce) package dried rice noodles
- 4 cups cold water, as needed
- ½ cup peanut oil
- 4 large eggs eggs
- 1 ½ teaspoons minced garlic
- 12 ounces chicken breast, cut into 1/2-inch strips
- 1 ½ tablespoons white sugar, or more to taste
- 1 ½ teaspoons salt
- 1 ½ cups dry-roasted, unsalted peanuts
- 1 ½ teaspoons dried ground Asian radish
- 1 teaspoon chili powder, or more to taste
- ½ cup chopped fresh chives
- 2 cups fresh bean sprouts
- 1 lime, cut into wedges

Directions

- **Step 1**
Whisk together rice wine vinegar, 1/2 cup sugar, oyster sauce, and tamarind pulp in a saucepan over medium heat until sugar dissolves, about 5 minutes; remove from heat and set aside.

- **Step 2**

Place rice noodles in a large bowl and pour enough cold water to cover noodles. Allow to soften, about 10 minutes. Drain.

- **Step 3**

Heat peanut oil in a wok or large skillet over medium heat. Cook and stir eggs and garlic in hot oil until eggs are softly cooked, 2 to 3 minutes.

- **Step 4**

Stir chicken and noodles into eggs and cook until chicken is no longer pink in the center and juices run clear, about 5 minutes.

- **Step 5**
Pour rice wine vinegar sauce, 1 1/2 tablespoons sugar, and 1 1/2 teaspoons salt into the noodle mixture.
- **Step 6**
Stir peanuts, ground radish, and chili powder into noodle mixture; cook until peanuts soften slightly, about 5 minutes. Add more sugar or chili powder if desired.
- **Step 7**
Remove from heat and toss chives with noodle mixture. Top with bean sprouts and garnish with lime wedges.

Nutrition Facts
Per Serving:
596.7 calories; protein 21.1g 42% DV; carbohydrates 61.6g 20% DV; fat 31g 48% DV; cholesterol 117.2mg 39% DV; sodium 635.3mg 25% DV.

Monica's Japanese Garlic Dollop Shrimp

Prep: 20 mins **Cook:** 5 mins **Additional:** 1 hr **Total:** 1 hr 25 mins **Servings:** 4 **Yield:** 4 servings

Ingredients
- ¾ cup mayonnaise
- 2 tablespoons soy sauce
- 2 tablespoons mirin
- 2 cloves garlic, minced
- 2 tablespoons dried minced onion
- ¼ teaspoon onion powder
- 1 teaspoon curry powder
- 1 teaspoon ground turmeric
- 1 teaspoon dried basil
- 1 tablespoon cayenne pepper
- ¼ teaspoon salt
- ½ cup seasoned dry bread crumbs
- 16 eaches peeled and deveined jumbo shrimp, tails still attached
- 2 tablespoons sesame oil
- ¼ cup water

Directions
- **Step 1**

Stir together the mayonnaise, soy sauce, mirin, minced garlic, dried minced onion, onion powder, curry powder, turmeric, basil, cayenne pepper, and salt in a bowl. Fold in the bread crumbs until evenly moistened. Cover, and refrigerate at least an hour.

- **Step 2**

Cut each shrimp along the back and open the halves like a book. Place a hearty dollop of the mayonnaise mixture onto each shrimp, and spread over the top to completely cover. Heat the sesame oil in a large skillet over high heat until it begins to smoke. Place the shrimp in the pan, mayonnaise-side up, and add the water. Cover, and steam until the shrimp are no longer transparent, 2 1/2 to 3 minutes.

Nutrition Facts

Per Serving:

560.4 calories; protein 26.5g 53% DV; carbohydrates 18.1g 6% DV; fat 41.9g 65% DV; cholesterol 229mg 76% DV; sodium 1341.5mg 54% DV.

Curry Tofu Stir-Fry

Prep: 10 mins **Cook:** 25 mins **Total:** 35 mins **Servings:** 4 **Yield:** 4 main-dish servings

Ingredients

- 1 serving cooking spray
- 1 pound extra-firm tofu, cut into 1-inch cubes
- 1 tablespoon vegetable oil
- 1 cup sliced fresh mushrooms
- 1 tablespoon chopped garlic
- 3 cups fresh spinach
- 2 tablespoons soy sauce
- 1 ½ tablespoons curry powder
- 1 teaspoon red pepper flakes

Directions

- **Step 1**

Preheat oven to 400 degrees F (200 degrees C). Spray a baking sheet with baking spray; arrange tofu in a single layer.

- **Step 2**

Bake tofu in preheated oven until evenly browned, flipping after 10 minutes, about 20 minutes total.

- **Step 3**

Heat vegetable oil in a wok or large skillet over medium-high heat. Add mushrooms and garlic; cook and stir until mushrooms are tender; 2 to 3 minutes. Add tofu, spinach, soy sauce, and curry powder; cook and stir until spinach is wilted; 3 to 5 minutes. Sprinkle red pepper flakes over mixture.

Nutrition Facts

Per Serving:

142.8 calories; protein 11.4g 23% DV; carbohydrates 6.6g 2% DV; fat 9.4g 15% DV; cholesterolmg; sodium 480.3mg 19% DV.

Bekki's Mexican Egg Rolls

Prep: 20 mins **Cook:** 30 mins **Additional:** 15 mins **Total:** 1 hr 5 mins **Servings:** 10 **Yield:** 20 egg rolls

Ingredients

- 2 tablespoons vegetable oil
- 1 pound ground beef
- 1 large onion, chopped
- 5 cloves garlic, minced
- 1 red bell pepper, chopped
- 1 (1 ounce) package taco seasoning
- 1 (8 ounce) jar taco sauce
- 4 (16 ounce) packages egg roll wrappers
- 1 (1 pound) loaf processed cheese food (i.e. Velveeta®), cut into 1/4 inch thick slices
- 2 large egg whites egg whites, lightly beaten
- 2 quarts canola oil

Directions

- **Step 1**

    Place the vegetable oil and ground beef into a large skillet; cook over medium-high heat until the meat is evenly browned and no longer pink. Reduce the heat to medium. Mix in the onion, garlic, and bell pepper; cook until the vegetables are softened, about 5 minutes. Stir in the taco seasoning and taco sauce. Continue to cook and stir the mixture until the sauce begins to bubble, about 5 minutes more.

- **Step 2**

    Working on a clean, flat surface, place 1 egg roll wrapper with a corner facing you. Place 1 tablespoon of the meat mixture in the center of the wrapper and top with a slice of cheese. Fold the corner closest to you over the meat mixture and roll the wrapper over the mixture 1-1/2 times. Fold in the two opposite side corners and continue rolling the wrapper so it covers these corners, tucking them in. Dip two fingers in the egg whites and brush the remaining corner, pressing it to seal. Repeat these steps with a second egg roll wrapper. Let the egg roll rest briefly so the egg white dries and holds the last corner in place.

- **Step 3**

    If the egg rolls will not be served right away, preheat oven to 325 degrees F (165 degrees C). Line a heat-proof dish with paper towels.

- **Step 4**

    Pour the canola oil into a large wok set over medium-high heat. When the oil begins to shimmer, carefully slip two to three egg rolls into the wok. Cook until the wrappers turn golden brown and bubble slightly, 30 seconds to 1 minute. Use a slotted spoon or strainer to remove from the wok. Place the egg rolls in the prepared dish and put the dish in the heated oven, making sure to remove it after 15 minute or lower the temperature. Continue cooking the remaining egg rolls.

Note

It is very important to use TWO egg roll wrappers and wrap them twice around the filling, tucking in the corners each time. If the egg roll is not double-wrapped and sealed, its contents will leak out when cooked.

Nutrition Facts

Per Serving:

979.9 calories; protein 34.4g 69% DV; carbohydrates 113.3g 37% DV; fat 41.7g 64% DV; cholesterol 79.8mg 27% DV; sodium 1971.9mg 79% DV.

Spicy Green Beans and Pork, Asian Style

Prep: 20 mins **Cook:** 15 mins **Total:** 35 mins **Servings:** 4 **Yield:** 4 servings

Ingredients

- 2 cups vegetable oil for frying
- 1 pound fresh green beans, trimmed and dried well with paper towels
- Pork Sauce:
- 1 tablespoon vegetable oil
- 3 cloves garlic, minced
- 2 teaspoons minced fresh ginger root
- 2 eaches green onions, minced
- ½ pound ground pork
- 2 tablespoons Asian chili garlic sauce
- ¼ cup chicken broth
- 2 teaspoons soy sauce
- 2 teaspoons cornstarch
- 2 tablespoons cold water

Directions

- **Step 1**

    Heat 2 cups of vegetable oil in a large wok or deep sided skillet to 375 degrees F (190 degrees C). Carefully add the beans to the hot oil, and fry, stirring occasionally, until the beans are blistered, 3 to 5 minutes. Dip the beans out of the oil with a strainer, and quickly rinse them in cold water.

- **Step 2**

    Remove the oil from the wok, but do not wipe the pan. Heat 1 tablespoon of vegetable oil in the wok over medium heat, and stir in the garlic, ginger, and green onion. Cook and stir until fragrant, about 30 seconds, and stir in the ground pork. Cook and stir the pork, breaking it up as it cooks, until no longer pink, about 4 minutes. Stir in the chili garlic sauce, chicken broth, and soy sauce, and bring to a boil.

- **Step 3**

    Mix the cornstarch with the water in a small bowl, stir into the pork mixture, and let simmer until the sauce thickens, 1 to 2 minutes. Gently stir the green beans into the pork sauce, heat through, and serve.

Cook's Note

It is important to use an Asian/Chinese Style chili garlic sauce in this recipe (found in almost all Chinese/International sections of stores, or buy from web sites). Fresh garlic, ginger and onions are also key to an authentic taste.

Nutrition Facts

Per Serving:

295.1 calories; protein 12.6g 25% DV; carbohydrates 11.7g 4% DV; fat 22.7g 35% DV; cholesterol 36.7mg 12% DV; sodium 504.2mg 20% DV.

Chinese Braised Zucchini

Prep: 30 mins **Cook:** 20 mins **Total:** 50 mins **Servings:** 4 **Yield:** 4 servings

Ingredients

- 2 tablespoons sesame oil
- 1 small yellow onion, diced
- 3 cloves garlic, minced
- 1 tablespoon Chinese black bean sauce
- 2 peppers Thai chile peppers, seeded and chopped
- 4 medium (blank)s zucchinis, cut into 1/2-inch slices
- 1 tablespoon minced fresh ginger root
- 1 tablespoon soy sauce
- ¼ cup water

Directions

- **Step 1**

    Heat the sesame oil in a wok or large skillet over medium-high heat. Stir fry the onion and garlic in the hot oil until the onion begins to soften, about 2 minutes. Stir in the black bean sauce and chile peppers, and continue stir frying about 30 seconds to coat the onions with the black bean sauce.

- **Step 2**

    Stir in the zucchini, ginger, soy sauce, and water. Cover, reduce the heat to medium-low, and cook for 15 minutes until the zucchini is soft, stirring occasionally.

Nutrition Facts

Per Serving:

118.1 calories; protein 3.5g 7% DV; carbohydrates 12.1g 4% DV; fat 7.4g 11% DV; cholesterolmg; sodium 275.5mg 11% DV.

Easy Japanese-Style Vegan Collard Greens

Prep: 10 mins **Cook:** 5 mins **Total:** 15 mins **Servings:** 6 **Yield:** 6 servings

Ingredients

- 2 tablespoons Asian (toasted) sesame oil
- 1 bunch collard greens, thinly sliced
- 3 tablespoons gomasio (such as Eden Organic Foods®)
- 1 tablespoon mirin (Japanese sweet wine)
- 2 cloves garlic, minced, or more to taste
- 1 pinch sea salt to taste

Directions

- **Step 1**

  Heat sesame oil in a large skillet or wok until sizzling; add collard greens, gomasio, and mirin. Cook until collard greens are tender, 3 to 5 minutes.

- **Step 2**

  Stir garlic into collard green mixture and cook just until garlic is fragrant, about 30 seconds; remove from heat. Season with additional sea salt if desired.

Cook's Notes:

If you cannot find gomasio, simply buy sesame seeds and toast them lightly in a dry skillet. Then transfer seeds to a spice grinder or mortar and pestle and coarsely grind with a ratio of 1/4 cup sesame seeds to 1 teaspoon sea salt.

I prefer to cook the collard greens at a medium-high temp for a short period of time, thereby preserving the pungent flavor of the greens.

Onion can be added to this dish if fried for five minutes before adding the collards, but I enjoy the character of this dish without them.

Nutrition Facts
Per Serving:

85.3 calories; protein 2.7g 5% DV; carbohydrates 5.3g 2% DV; fat 7.1g 11% DV; cholesterolmg; sodium 183.1mg 7% DV.

Apple Fried Rice

Prep: 30 mins **Cook:** 25 mins **Total:** 55 mins **Servings:** 4 **Yield:** 4 servings

Ingredients

- 6 ounces shrimp - peeled, veined, and cut into 1-inch pieces
- 1 pinch salt and ground black pepper to taste
- 1 teaspoon cornstarch
- 1 tablespoon vegetable oil, or more as needed
- 1 teaspoon minced garlic
- 1 egg, beaten
- 1 cup diced button mushrooms
- ¾ cup frozen mixed vegetables
- 1 apple - peeled, cored, and diced
- 2 tablespoons raisins
- 1 teaspoon curry powder
- 1 tablespoon light soy sauce
- 2 cups overnight steamed white rice
- 1 green onion, diced

Directions
- **Step 1**
  Mix shrimp, salt, and pepper together in a bowl; stir in cornstarch.
- **Step 2**
  Heat oil in a wok over medium heat; add shrimp mixture. Cook until light brown, about 5 minutes. Transfer to a plate.
- **Step 3**
  Stir garlic into the wok; cook until fragrant, about 1 minute. Add egg; cook and stir until scrambled, about 3 minutes. Mix in mushrooms; cook and stir until softened, about 5 minutes.
- **Step 4**
  Stir mixed vegetables into the wok; cook until softened, 3 to 5 minutes. Mix in apple and raisins; add curry powder. Cook and stir until fragrant, about 3 minutes.
- **Step 5**
  Mix rice into the wok; season with soy sauce, salt, and pepper. Cook and stir until rice is heated through, 3 to 5 minutes. Add shrimp and green onion; cook and stir until warmed through, 2 to 4 minutes.

Cook's Notes:
Shrimp can be substituted with processed meats (such as wieners, luncheon meat, or ham), leftover diced turkey, or 1/4 pound ground pork or chicken.

If substituting shrimp with ground pork or chicken, season with 1/4 teaspoon each salt and pepper and 1 teaspoon each cornstarch and sesame oil.

Nutrition Facts
Per Serving:
247.7 calories; protein 12.7g 26% DV; carbohydrates 37.5g 12% DV; fat 5.6g 9% DV; cholesterol 110.4mg 37% DV; sodium 371mg 15% DV.

Pad Thai with Spaghetti Squash

Prep: 20 mins **Cook:** 55 mins **Additional:** 1 hr **Total:** 2 hrs 15 mins **Servings:** 4 **Yield:** 4 servings

Ingredients

- 1 (12 ounce) package extra-firm tofu
- 1 spaghetti squash, halved lengthwise
- 6 tablespoons sesame oil, divided
- 2 large eggs eggs
- ¼ cup cornstarch
- 2 cups bean sprouts
- 6 tablespoons pad Thai sauce
- 1 tablespoon Thai garlic chile paste
- 4 eaches green onions, thinly sliced
- 1 cup cashew pieces

Directions

- **Step 1**

  Drain tofu and slice horizontally into 1/4-inch slices. Lay paper towels on a cutting board, place tofu slices on top, and cover with another layer of paper towels. Place something heavy, such as a cast iron skillet, on top. Allow to drain for 1 to 2 hours.

- **Step 2**

  Preheat oven to 450 degrees F (230 degrees C). Place spaghetti squash, cut-side up, on a baking sheet.

- **Step 3**

  Bake spaghetti squash in preheated oven until tender, 45 to 50 minutes. Remove squash from oven; remove and separate strands from peel using a fork.

- **Step 4**

  Heat 2 tablespoons sesame oil in wok or large skillet over medium-high heat. Add eggs, cook and stir until eggs are cooked through and scrambles, about 5 minutes. Transfer eggs to a plate.

- **Step 5**

  Cut each slice of tofu into 9 triangles and place in a bowl; add cornstarch and toss to coat. Shake tofu to remove excess cornstarch.

- **Step 6**

  Heat remaining 4 tablespoons sesame oil in wok over medium-high heat; add tofu and saute until crispy, about 5 minutes. Remove from wok. Place squash, bean sprouts, Pad Thai sauce, garlic chile paste, and onions into wok and saute until heated through, about 10 minutes. Mix tofu and scrambled eggs into squash mixture. Remove wok from heat, add cashews, and toss to combine.

Nutrition Facts

Per Serving:

617.4 calories; protein 17.8g 36% DV; carbohydrates 45.5g 15% DV; fat 43.9g 68% DV; cholesterol 93mg 31% DV; sodium 427.4mg 17% DV.

Pineapple Fried Rice with Ham

Prep: 15 mins **Cook:** 10 mins **Total:** 25 mins **Servings:** 4 **Yield:** 4 servings

Ingredients

- 3 tablespoons soy sauce
- 1 tablespoon sesame oil
- ½ teaspoon ground ginger
- ¼ teaspoon white pepper
- 2 tablespoons olive oil
- 1 onion, diced
- 2 cloves garlic, minced
- 2 carrot, (7-1/2")s carrots, peeled and grated
- ½ cup frozen corn
- ½ cup frozen peas
- 3 cups cooked brown rice
- 2 cups diced pineapple
- ½ cup diced ham
- 2 medium (4-1/8" long)s green onions, sliced

Directions

- **Step 1**

  Whisk soy sauce, sesame oil, ground ginger, and white pepper together in a bowl; set aside.

- **Step 2**

  Heat olive oil in a large skillet or wok over medium-high heat. Add onion and cook, stirring often, until soft and translucent, 3 to 4 minutes. Add garlic and cook for an additional 30 seconds. Stir in carrots, corn, and peas and stir-fry until vegetables are tender, 3 to 4 minutes.

- **Step 3**

  Stir in brown rice, pineapple, ham, green onions, and soy sauce mixture. Cook, stirring constantly, until heated through, about 2 minutes. Serve immediately.

Nutrition Facts

Per Serving:

390.9 calories; protein 9.4g 19% DV; carbohydrates 60.9g 20% DV; fat 13.3g 21% DV; cholesterol 8.4mg 3% DV; sodium 916.6mg 37% DV.

Muscat Gosht (Lamb in Spicy Tomato Gravy)

Prep: 15 mins **Cook:** 45 mins **Total:** 1 hr **Servings:** 4 **Yield:** 4 servings

Ingredients

- 2 ¼ pounds boneless lamb shoulder, cut into 1 1/2 inch pieces
- 3 medium (2-1/2" dia)s onions, sliced
- 1 ¾ cups chopped tomato
- 1 ⅔ tablespoons garlic paste
- 1 ⅔ tablespoons ginger paste
- 1 tablespoon black peppercorns
- 1 (3 inch) cinnamon stick
- ¼ cup dried chile de arbol peppers
- 5 eaches whole clove
- 1 teaspoon black cardamom seeds
- 9 tablespoons ghee (clarified butter)
- 1 tablespoon salt

Directions

- **Step 1**

Place a large wok or skillet over low heat. Combine the lamb, onion, tomato, garlic paste, ginger paste, peppercorns, cinnamon, dried peppers, cloves, cardamom seeds, and salt in the pan and stir; cover and cook until the mutton is tender, 30 to 35 minutes. Stir in the ghee. Cook until the sauce has thickened, 10 to 15 minutes.

Nutrition Facts

Per Serving:

723.5 calories; protein 35.2g 70% DV; carbohydrates 14.8g 5% DV; fat 55.3g 85% DV; cholesterol 204.3mg 68% DV; sodium 2265.6mg 91% DV.

Vegetarian, Tofu-Less Stir-Fry

Prep: 10 mins **Cook:** 7 mins **Total:** 17 mins **Servings:** 2 **Yield:** 2 servings

Ingredients

- ¼ cup frozen shelled edamame (green soybeans)
- ⅛ teaspoon salt
- 1 tablespoon olive oil
- 1 clove garlic, minced
- 1 cup sliced yellow bell pepper
- ½ cup sliced yellow onion
- ½ cup bean sprouts
- 1 tablespoon tamari soy sauce

- 2 cups cooked pasta
- 1 tablespoon sesame oil
- 1 teaspoon toasted sesame seeds

Directions

- **Step 1**

    Stir edamame and salt together in a microwave-safe dish; cover and cook in microwave for 1 minute.

- **Step 2**

    Heat olive oil in a large wok over medium heat; add garlic and cook until fragrant and beginning to sizzle, about 1 minute. Add bell pepper and onion; cook and stir until beginning to brown, about 2 minutes. Add bean sprouts and soy sauce; cook and stir until soy sauce begins to evaporate, about 1 minute. Add edamame, cooked pasta, sesame oil, and sesame seeds; stir until cooked through, about 30 seconds.

Cook's Note:

I buy a lot of the ingredients (cooked pasta, sliced peppers, and onions) pre-prepared, so that it doesn't take a long time to prepare.

Nutrition Facts

Per Serving:

399.2 calories; protein 11.1g 22% DV; carbohydrates 54.2g 18% DV; fat 15.8g 24% DV; cholesterolmg; sodium 654.2mg 26% DV.

Kristy's Le Tofu Orange

Prep: 30 mins **Cook:** 19 mins **Additional:** 10 mins **Total:** 59 mins **Servings:** 4 **Yield:** 4 servings

Ingredients

- 1 (14 ounce) package baked firm tofu, cut into 1-inch cubes
- 2 tablespoons olive oil, or as needed, divided
- 12 ounces riced cauliflower (such as Trader Joe's®)
- 2 medium (2-1/2" dia)s onions, chopped
- 3 eaches scallions, chopped
- 2 cloves garlic, minced
- 2 medium (blank)s green bell peppers, chopped
- 2 tablespoons water
- 1 tablespoon orange liqueur (such as Grand Marnier®)
- 1 tablespoon soy sauce
- 2 eaches red chile peppers, shredded
- 1 pinch salt

Directions

- **Step 1**

Wrap tofu in a paper towel and cover with plate; rest until moisture is removed, about 10 minutes.

- **Step 2**

  Heat 1 tablespoon olive oil in a skillet over medium heat. Add cauliflower; cook and stir until tender, about 5 minutes.

- **Step 3**

  Preheat oven to 425 degrees F (220 degrees C). (If using a countertop convection oven, preheat to 400 degrees F (200 degrees C)). Place baking sheet inside to warm.

- **Step 4**

  Remove paper towel from tofu; discard. Place tofu onto heated baking sheet using heatproof gloves.

- **Step 5**

  Bake in the preheated oven, flipping once, until tofu is heated through, about 3 minutes per side in the conventional oven and 2 minutes per side in the countertop induction oven.

- **Step 6**

  Heat remaining 1 tablespoon olive oil in a wok on medium heat. Add onions and scallions; cook and stir until onions are slightly softened, about 5 minutes. Stir in garlic. Turn wok to high heat; stir in green peppers.

- **Step 7**

  Combine water and orange liqueur in a bowl. Pour 1 tablespoon liqueur mixture into wok; toss with 2 wooden spoons until mixed. Repeat with remaining liqueur mixture; cook and stir until evaporated, 3 to 5 minutes.

- **Step 8**

  Sprinkle soy sauce into the wok. Fold in tofu until coated.

- **Step 9**

  Place cauliflower in serving bowls and top with tofu mixture. Garnish with red chile peppers; season with salt.

Nutrition Facts

Per Serving:

298.6 calories; protein 19.3g 39% DV; carbohydrates 21.1g 7% DV; fat 15.7g 24% DV; cholesterolmg; sodium 779mg 31% DV.

Summer Special Shrimp and Fruit Fried Rice

Prep: 40 mins **Cook:** 20 mins **Total:** 1 hr **Servings:** 2 **Yield:** 2 servings

Ingredients

- 1 tablespoon vegetable oil, divided
- 2 large eggs eggs, beaten
- ½ pound peeled and deveined medium shrimp
- 1 (1 inch) piece fresh ginger root, minced
- 2 eaches red onions, sliced

- 3 eaches green chile peppers, chopped
- ⅔ cup fresh pineapple, diced
- ½ cup orange segments
- 6 halves walnuts, chopped
- 2 cups cold, cooked white rice
- 1 tablespoon soy sauce
- 2 tablespoons chopped fresh cilantro
- 1 pinch salt and pepper to taste

Directions

- **Step 1**

  Heat 1 teaspoon of the vegetable oil in a wok over medium-high heat. Pour in the onions, and cook until just set; set aside. Increase the heat to high, and pour another 1 teaspoon of oil to the wok. Stir in the shrimp, and cook until the shrimp turn pink, and are no longer translucent in the center, about 3 minutes; set aside.

- **Step 2**

  Wipe out the wok, and heat the remaining teaspoon of oil over high heat. Stir in the ginger, and cook quickly for a few seconds until the ginger begins to turn golden brown. Stir in the onion and chile peppers; cook for a minute or two until the onions begin to soften and turn brown around the edges. Add the pineapple and oranges, and gently cook until the pineapple is hot.

- **Step 3**

  Stir in the rice, walnuts, and soy sauce. Stir for a few minutes until the rice is hot. Fold in the egg, shrimp, and cilantro. Season to taste with salt and pepper, and cook to reheat.

Nutrition Facts

Per Serving:

590.8 calories; protein 33.9g 68% DV; carbohydrates 76.1g 25% DV; fat 17.5g 27% DV; cholesterol 358.6mg 120% DV; sodium 732.3mg 29% DV.

Balsamic Vinegar and Ginger Bok Choy

Prep: 15 mins **Cook:** 15 mins **Total:** 30 mins **Servings:** 4 **Yield:** 4 servings

Ingredients

- 4 heads baby bok choy
- 3 tablespoons olive oil
- ¼ cup water
- 2 tablespoons capers
- 1 ½ teaspoons minced garlic
- 1 ½ teaspoons minced fresh ginger root
- 2 tablespoons balsamic vinegar

- 1 dash fresh lemon juice, or to taste

Directions

- **Step 1**

  Separate the leaves from the stems of the bok choy. Cut the stems into bite-sized chunks and shred the leaves.

- **Step 2**

  Heat the olive oil in large skillet over medium heat.

- **Step 3**

  Cook the bok choy stems in the oil until slightly tender, about 3 minutes; add the water and leaves and cook until the water evaporates, about 10 minutes more. Stir in the capers, garlic, and ginger; cook and stir 1 minute more. Sprinkle the vinegar and lemon juice over the bok choy and remove from heat; serve immediately.

Nutrition Facts

Per Serving:

110.8 calories; protein 1.7g 3% DV; carbohydrates 4.1g 1% DV; fat 10.4g 16% DV; cholesterolmg; sodium 195.3mg 8% DV.

Honey-Ginger Shrimp and Vegetables

Prep: 30 mins **Cook:** 15 mins **Total:** 45 mins **Servings:** 4 **Yield:** 4 servings

Ingredients

- 2 tablespoons olive oil
- 3 cloves garlic, minced
- ½ onion, chopped
- 1 ½ teaspoons ground ginger
- 2 teaspoons red pepper flakes
- 1 red bell pepper, chopped
- ½ zucchini, halved lengthwise and sliced
- 3 cups fresh mushrooms, coarsely chopped
- 2 tablespoons cornstarch
- ½ cup honey
- 1 pound medium shrimp - peeled and deveined
- 1 pinch salt and pepper to taste

Directions

- **Step 1**

  Heat olive oil in a wok or large skillet over high heat until it begins to smoke. Stir in garlic, onion, ginger, and red pepper flakes. Quickly cook until the onion softens and just begins to brown. Stir in bell pepper, zucchini, and mushrooms; continue cooking until the zucchini softens, about 4 minutes.

- **Step 2**

    Stir cornstarch into honey until smooth, then add to vegetables, and simmer until thickened, about 2 minutes. Add shrimp, and cook until they turn pink, about 3 minutes. Season to taste with salt and pepper before serving.

Nutrition Facts

Per Serving:

369 calories; protein 26g 52% DV; carbohydrates 48.3g 16% DV; fat 9.3g 14% DV; cholesterol 172.5mg 58% DV; sodium 177.6mg 7% DV.

Shrimp Lo Mein with Broccoli

Prep: 10 mins **Cook:** 25 mins **Total:** 35 mins **Servings:** 2 **Yield:** 2 servings

Ingredients

- 1 (8 ounce) package spaghetti
- 2 tablespoons soy sauce
- 2 tablespoons oyster sauce
- 2 tablespoons brown sugar
- 2 teaspoons fish sauce
- ½ teaspoon garlic powder
- ½ teaspoon ground ginger
- 2 teaspoons vegetable oil
- 1 pound uncooked medium shrimp, peeled and deveined
- 1 cup chopped broccoli
- ¼ yellow onion, thinly sliced
- 3 medium (blank)s crimini mushrooms, sliced
- 2 cloves garlic, minced
- 2 large eggs large eggs

Directions

- **Step 1**

    Bring a large pot of lightly salted water to a boil. Cook spaghetti in the boiling water until cooked through yet firm to the bite, about 12 minutes; drain.

- **Step 2**

    Mix soy sauce, oyster sauce, brown sugar, fish sauce, garlic powder, and ground ginger in a bowl until the sugar dissolves.

- **Step 3**

    Heat oil in a large skillet or wok over medium heat; cook and stir shrimp in hot oil until they start to change color, 1 to 2 minutes. Add broccoli, onion, and mushrooms; cook until just beginning to soften, 3 to 5 minutes. Stir garlic through the vegetable mixture. Push the vegetables to one side of the pan. Cook the eggs in the clear space in the pan, scrambling lightly, until no longer moist, 3 to 5 minutes. Stir the cooked egg with shrimp and vegetables. Add the cooked noodles and the sauce; cook and stir until hot and evenly mixed, about 2 minutes more. Serve immediately.

Nutrition Facts

Per Serving:

833.8 calories; protein 63.9g 128% DV; carbohydrates 109.5g 35% DV; fat 14.3g 22% DV; cholesterol 531.2mg 177% DV; sodium 2240mg 90% DV.

'Chinese Buffet' Green Beans

Prep: 15 mins **Cook:** 10 mins **Total:** 25 mins **Servings:** 6 **Yield:** 6 servings

Ingredients

- 1 tablespoon oil, peanut or sesame
- 2 cloves garlic, thinly sliced
- 1 pound fresh green beans, trimmed
- 1 tablespoon white sugar
- 2 tablespoons oyster sauce
- 2 teaspoons soy sauce

Directions

- **Step 1**

Heat peanut oil in a wok or large skillet over medium-high heat. Stir in the garlic, and cook until the edges begin to brown, about 20 seconds. Add the green beans; cook and stir until the green beans begin to soften, about 5 minutes. Stir in the sugar, oyster sauce, and soy sauce. Continue cooking and stirring for several minutes until the beans have attained the desired degree of tenderness.

Nutrition Facts

Per Serving:

54.5 calories; protein 1.6g 3% DV; carbohydrates 8.1g 3% DV; fat 2.3g 4% DV; cholesterolmg; sodium 140.7mg 6% DV.

Super Easy Stir-Fried Cabbage

Prep: 10 mins **Cook:** 5 mins **Total:** 15 mins **Servings:** 4 **Yield:** 4 servings

Ingredients

- 1 tablespoon vegetable oil
- 2 cloves garlic, minced
- 1 pound shredded cabbage
- 1 tablespoon soy sauce
- 1 tablespoon Chinese cooking wine (Shaoxing wine)

Directions
- **Step 1**

  Heat the vegetable oil in a wok or large skillet over medium heat. Stir in the garlic, and cook for a few seconds until it begins to brown. Stir in the cabbage until it is coated in oil; cover the wok, and cook for 1 minute. Pour in the soy sauce, and cook and stir for another minute. Increase the heat to high, and stir in the Chinese cooking wine. Cook and stir until the cabbage is tender, about 2 minutes more.

Tips

Cook's Note

I prefer to use a gas stove for this recipe.

Nutrition Facts

Per Serving:

64.7 calories; protein 1.8g 4% DV; carbohydrates 7.4g 2% DV; fat 3.5g 5% DV; cholesterolmg; sodium 269.9mg 11% DV.

Zucchini Noodles Pad Thai

Prep: 45 mins **Cook:** 12 mins **Total:** 57 mins **Servings:** 4 **Yield:** 4 servings

Ingredients
- 3 large zucchini
- ¼ cup chicken stock
- 2 ½ tablespoons tamarind paste
- 2 tablespoons low-sodium soy sauce
- 2 tablespoons oyster sauce
- 1 ½ tablespoons Asian chile pepper sauce
- 1 tablespoon Worcestershire sauce
- 1 tablespoon fresh lime juice
- 1 tablespoon white sugar
- 2 tablespoons sesame oil
- 1 tablespoon chopped garlic
- 12 ounces skinless, boneless chicken breasts, cut into 1-inch cubes
- 8 ounces peeled and deveined shrimp
- 2 large eggs eggs, beaten
- 2 tablespoons water, or as needed
- 3 cups bean sprouts, divided
- 6 eaches green onions, chopped into 1-inch pieces
- 2 tablespoons chopped unsalted dry-roasted peanuts
- ¼ cup chopped fresh basil

Directions

- **Step 1**

  Make zucchini noodles using a spiralizer.

- **Step 2**

  Whisk chicken stock, tamarind paste, soy sauce, oyster sauce, chile pepper sauce, Worcestershire sauce, lime juice, and sugar together in a small bowl to make a smooth sauce.

- **Step 3**

  Heat sesame oil in a wok or large skillet over high heat. Add garlic and stir until fragrant, about 10 seconds. Add chicken and shrimp; cook and stir until chicken is no longer pink in the center and the juices run clear, 5 to 7 minutes.

- **Step 4**

  Push chicken and shrimp to the sides of the wok to make a space in the center. Pour eggs and scramble until firm, 2 to 3 minutes. Add zucchini noodles and sauce; cook and stir, adding water if needed, about 3 minutes. Add 2 cups bean sprouts and green onions; cook and stir until combined, 1 to 2 minutes.

- **Step 5**

  Remove wok from heat and sprinkle peanuts over noodles. Serve garnished with remaining 1 cup bean sprouts and fresh basil.

Nutrition Facts

Per Serving:

370.2 calories; protein 35.6g 71% DV; carbohydrates 28.1g 9% DV; fat 14.5g 22% DV; cholesterol 221.8mg 74% DV; sodium 670.9mg 27% DV.

Authentic Pad Thai Noodles

Prep: 30 mins **Cook:** 20 mins **Additional:** 1 hr 10 mins **Total:** 2 hrs **Servings:** 4 **Yield:** 4 servings

Ingredients

- ⅔ cup dried rice vermicelli
- ¼ cup peanut oil
- ⅔ cup thinly sliced firm tofu
- 1 large egg, beaten
- 4 cloves garlic, finely chopped
- ¼ cup vegetable broth
- 2 tablespoons fresh lime juice
- 2 tablespoons soy sauce
- 1 tablespoon white sugar
- 1 teaspoon salt
- ½ teaspoon dried red chili flakes
- 3 tablespoons chopped peanuts
- 1 pound bean sprouts, divided

- 3 eaches green onions, whites cut thinly across and greens sliced into thin lengths - divided
- 3 tablespoons chopped peanuts
- 2 small (blank)s limes, cut into wedges for garnish

Directions

- **Step 1**

    Soak rice vermicelli noodles in a bowl filled with hot water until softened, 30 minutes to 1 hour. Drain and set aside.

- **Step 2**

    Heat peanut oil over medium heat in a large wok.

- **Step 3**

    Cook and stir tofu in the wok, turning the pieces until they are golden on all sides.

- **Step 4**

    Remove tofu with a slotted spoon and drain on plate lined with paper towels.

- **Step 5**

    Pour all but 1 tablespoon of used oil from the wok into a small bowl; it will be used again in a later step.

- **Step 6**

    Heat the remaining 1 tablespoon of oil in the wok over medium heat until it starts to sizzle.

- **Step 7**

    Pour in beaten egg and lightly toss in the hot oil to scramble the egg.

- **Step 8**

    Remove egg from the wok and set aside.

- **Step 9**

    Pour reserved peanut oil in the small bowl back into the wok.

- **Step 10**

    Toss garlic and drained noodles in wok until they are coated with oil.

- **Step 11**

    Stir in vegetable broth, lime juice, soy sauce, and sugar. Toss and gently push noodles around the pan to coat with sauce.

- **Step 12**

    Gently mix in tofu, scrambled egg, salt, chili flakes, and 3 tablespoons peanuts; toss to mix all ingredients.

- **Step 13**

    Mix in bean sprouts and green onions, reserving about 1 tablespoon of each for garnish. Cook and stir until bean sprouts have softened slightly, 1 to 2 minutes.

- **Step 14**

    Arrange noodles on a warm serving platter and garnish with 3 tablespoons peanuts and reserved bean sprouts and green onions. Place lime wedges around the edges of the platter.

Nutrition Facts

Per Serving:

396.8 calories; protein 13.2g 26% DV; carbohydrates 39.5g 13% DV; fat 23.3g 36% DV; cholesterol 40.9mg 14% DV; sodium 1233.8mg 49% DV.

Chicken and Snow Peas

Prep: 15 mins **Cook:** 15 mins **Total:** 30 mins **Servings:** 6 **Yield:** 6 servings

Ingredients

- 1 cup chicken broth
- 3 tablespoons soy sauce
- 1 tablespoon cornstarch
- 1 tablespoon ground ginger
- 2 tablespoons vegetable oil
- 4 large skinless, boneless chicken breast halves, cubed
- 2 cloves garlic, minced
- 1 ½ cups sliced fresh mushrooms
- 2 (8 ounce) cans sliced water chestnuts, drained
- 3 cups snow peas
- 1 tablespoon sesame seeds

Directions

- **Step 1**

  Whisk the chicken broth, soy sauce, cornstarch, and ginger together in a small bowl; reserve.

- **Step 2**

  Heat oil in a large skillet or wok. Cook and stir chicken and garlic in the oil until chicken is cooked through, 8 to 10 minutes. Stir in mushrooms, water chestnuts, and reserved chicken broth mixture. Cook until sauce begins to thicken, 3 to 5 minutes.

- **Step 3**

  Stir snow peas into the pan and cook until tender, 3 to 5 minutes. Transfer to a platter and sprinkle with sesame seeds before serving.

Nutrition Facts

Per Serving:

315.4 calories; protein 37.6g 75% DV; carbohydrates 17.3g 6% DV; fat 10.3g 16% DV; cholesterol 92.2mg 31% DV; sodium 540.9mg 22% DV.

Pork and Bamboo Shoots

Prep: 15 mins **Cook:** 15 mins **Total:** 30 mins **Servings:** 2 **Yield:** 2 servings

Ingredients

- 1 tablespoon peanut oil
- 1 (14 ounce) can thinly sliced bamboo shoots
- 2 tablespoons peanut oil
- 2 cloves garlic, minced
- 1 fresh red chile pepper, seeded and minced
- ½ teaspoon crushed red pepper flakes
- 3 ounces ground pork
- 1 teaspoon Shaoxing rice wine
- 1 pinch salt to taste
- 2 teaspoons rice vinegar
- 2 teaspoons soy sauce
- 3 tablespoons chicken broth
- 3 eaches green onions, thinly sliced
- 1 teaspoon sesame oil

Directions

- **Step 1**

  Heat one tablespoon peanut oil in a wok set over medium heat. Add the bamboo shoots to the pan; stir-fry until dry and fragrant, about 3 minutes. Remove from wok and reserve.

- **Step 2**

  Increase temperature to high, and pour in the remaining peanut oil. Quickly fry the garlic, red chile, and red pepper flakes in the hot oil until fragrant. Stir in the pork, and continue to stir-fry until it is cooked through. Pour in the wine; season with salt to taste.

- **Step 3**

  Return the bamboo shoots to the wok, and heat until sizzly. Stir in the rice vinegar, soy sauce, chicken broth, and additional salt to taste. Cook and stir for 1 to 2 minutes to allow the flavor to penetrate the bamboo shoots. At the end of cooking, stir in green onions. Remove wok from heat; stir in sesame oil before serving.

Cook's Notes:

Dry sherry can be substituted for the Shaoxing rice wine, if desired.

Water can be substituted for the chicken stock, if desired.

Nutrition Facts

Per Serving:

352.8 calories; protein 12.3g 25% DV; carbohydrates 11.9g 4% DV; fat 29.7g 46% DV; cholesterol 27.3mg 9% DV; sodium 340.1mg 14% DV.

Chicken Afritada (Filipino Stew)

Prep: 40 mins **Cook:** 48 mins **Total:** 1 hr 28 mins **Servings:** 6 **Yield:** 6 servings

Ingredients

- 1 tablespoon vegetable oil
- 3 cloves garlic, crushed and chopped
- 1 onion, chopped
- 1 cup seeded and chopped tomatoes
- 1 (3 pound) whole chicken, cut into pieces
- 3 cups water
- 1 cup tomato sauce
- 3 medium (2-1/4" to 3" dia, raw)s potatoes, quartered
- 1 green bell pepper, seeded and cut into matchsticks
- 1 carrot, chopped
- 1 pinch salt and ground black pepper to taste

Directions

- **Step 1**

  Heat oil in a large wok over medium heat; add garlic. Cook and stir until fragrant, about 3 minutes. Add onion; cook and stir until translucent, about 5 minutes. Stir in tomatoes; cook, mashing with a fork, until flesh and skin separate, about 5 minutes.

- **Step 2**

  Place chicken in the wok; cook and stir until lightly browned, about 5 minutes. Pour in water. Cover and bring to a boil. Stir in tomato sauce; simmer until flavors combine, about 15 minutes.

- **Step 3**

  Mix potatoes into the wok; simmer until tender, about 10 minutes. Stir in bell pepper and carrot; simmer until softened, about 5 minutes. Season with salt and pepper.

Nutrition Facts

Per Serving:

593.6 calories; protein 22.8g 46% DV; carbohydrates 25.1g 8% DV; fat 44.7g 69% DV; cholesterol 80.3mg 27% DV; sodium 324.2mg 13% DV.

Stir-Fried Mushrooms with Baby Corn

Prep: 10 mins **Cook:** 15 mins **Total:** 25 mins **Servings:** 4 **Yield:** 4 servings

Ingredients

- 2 tablespoons cooking oil
- 3 cloves garlic, minced
- 1 onion, diced
- 8 ears baby corn ears, sliced
- ⅔ pound fresh mushrooms, sliced
- 1 tablespoon fish sauce

- 1 tablespoon light soy sauce
- 1 tablespoon oyster sauce
- 2 teaspoons cornstarch
- 3 tablespoons water
- 1 red chile pepper, sliced
- ¼ cup chopped fresh cilantro

Directions

- **Step 1**

    Heat the oil in a large skillet or wok over medium heat; cook the garlic in the hot oil until browned, 5 to 7 minutes. Add the onion and baby corn and cook until the onion is translucent, 5 to 7 minutes. Add the mushrooms to the mixture and cook until slightly softened, about 2 minutes. Pour the fish sauce, soy sauce, and oyster sauce into the mixture and stir until incorporated.

- **Step 2**

    Whisk the cornstarch and water together in a small bowl until the cornstarch is dissolved into the water; pour into the mushroom mixture. Cook and stir until thickened and glistening. Transfer to a serving dish; garnish with the chile pepper and cilantro to serve.

Nutrition Facts

Per Serving:

48.8 calories; protein 3.4g 7% DV; carbohydrates 8.3g 3% DV; fat 0.9g 1% DV; cholesterolmg; sodium 448.2mg 18% DV.

Bitter Melon and Black Bean Sauce Beef

Prep: 20 mins **Cook:** 15 mins **Additional:** 1 hr **Total:** 1 hr 35 mins **Servings:** 4 **Yield:** 4 servings

Ingredients

- 1 ice cubes
- 1 bitter melon, seeded and sliced
- 2 teaspoons soy sauce, divided
- 2 teaspoons cornstarch, divided
- ¼ teaspoon baking soda
- 6 ounces beef, sliced
- 1 tablespoon oil
- 1 teaspoon oil
- ½ onion, sliced
- 2 cloves garlic
- 1 tablespoon chopped fresh ginger
- 1 tablespoon black bean sauce
- 1 tablespoon oyster sauce

- 1 pinch white sugar, or to taste
- ¾ cup water
- 1 teaspoon water
- 1 pinch salt to taste

Directions

- **Step 1**

  Fill a bowl with ice; add enough salted water to make an ice bath. Bring a large pot of lightly salted water to a boil. Cook the bitter melon in the boiling water until tender yet firm, about 2 minutes; strain the melon. Place the melon into the ice bath; allow to sit until bitterness is extracted, about 1 hour. Drain melon.

- **Step 2**

  Whisk 1 teaspoon soy sauce, 1 teaspoon cornstarch, and baking soda together in a bowl. Add beef and toss to evenly coat. Marinate in the refrigerator for 1 hour.

- **Step 3**

  Heat wok, or a large skillet, on high until smoking. Add 1 tablespoon oil. Lay beef evenly across the bottom of the wok; cook until browned, about 2 minutes per side. Remove beef. Pour in 1 teaspoon of oil; allow to heat. Add onion, garlic, and ginger; cook and stir until fragrant, about 30 seconds. Stir in bitter melon; cook until combined, about 1 minute.

- **Step 4**

  Stir black bean sauce into melon mixture. Stir in remaining soy sauce, oyster sauce, and sugar. Pour in 3/4 cup water; cover and let simmer until flavors combine, 2 to 3 minutes. Uncover and mix in remaining cornstarch and 1 teaspoon water and stir until thickened.

Nutrition Facts

Per Serving:

141.3 calories; protein 8.3g 17% DV; carbohydrates 7.6g 3% DV; fat 8.6g 13% DV; cholesterol 22.5mg 8% DV; sodium 340.2mg 14% DV.

Pork, Apple, and Ginger Stir-Fry with Hoisin Sauce

Prep: 20 mins **Cook:** 20 mins **Total:** 40 mins **Servings:** 3 **Yield:** 3 servings

Ingredients

- 2 tablespoons hoisin sauce
- 2 tablespoons brown sugar
- 6 tablespoons soy sauce
- ½ cup applesauce
- 1 pound pork loin, sliced and cut into thin strips

- 1 ½ tablespoons cornstarch
- 2 tablespoons peanut oil
- ½ teaspoon sesame oil
- 1 tablespoon chopped fresh ginger root
- 3 cups broccoli florets

Directions

- **Step 1**

  Whisk together the hoisin sauce, brown sugar, soy sauce, and applesauce in a small bowl; set aside.

- **Step 2**

  Combine the pork and cornstarch in a bowl. Mix until the cornstarch evenly coats the pork; set aside.

- **Step 3**

  Heat the peanut oil and sesame oil in a large skillet or wok over medium-high heat. Cook the pork in three separate batches in the hot oil until no longer pink in the middle, 2 to 3 minutes per batch. Remove pork to a plate lined with paper towels to drain, reserving the oil. Add the ginger to the skillet; cook and stir for 30 seconds. Stir in the broccoli and cook until tender. Return the pork to the skillet and pour in the sauce; toss to coat. Cook until all ingredients are hot.

Nutrition Facts

Per Serving:

447.9 calories; protein 29.3g 59% DV; carbohydrates 30.4g 10% DV; fat 23.7g 36% DV; cholesterol 73.8mg 25% DV; sodium 2062mg 83% DV.

Grapes and Rice Stir Fry

Prep: 15 mins **Cook:** 10 mins **Total:** 25 mins **Servings:** 4 **Yield:** 4 cups

Ingredients

- 1 tablespoon vegetable oil
- 1 cup sliced red grapes
- 1 cup cubed cooked chicken
- 2 cups cooked rice
- ¼ cup chicken broth

Directions

- **Step 1**

  Heat the vegetable oil in a wok or large skillet over medium high heat. Stir in the grapes and chicken; cook and stir until the chicken is hot, and the grapes are tender, about 3 minutes. Add the rice and chicken broth; continue cooking until the rice is hot, about 2 minutes more.

Cook's Note

Make this vegetarian by substituting marinated tofu for the chicken, and vegetable broth for the chicken broth.

Nutrition Facts
Per Serving:

225.6 calories; protein 12g 24% DV; carbohydrates 29.4g 10% DV; fat 6.5g 10% DV; cholesterol 26.3mg 9% DV; sodium 23.3mg 1% DV.

Spicy Beef Filet in Oyster Sauce

Prep: 15 mins **Cook:** 10 mins **Additional:** 40 mins **Total:** 1 hr 5 mins **Servings:** 4 **Yield:** 4 small servings

Ingredients

- 1 teaspoon vegetable oil
- 1 teaspoon oyster sauce
- ½ teaspoon cornstarch
- ¾ pound beef tenderloin, cut into 1/4 inch strips
- 1 teaspoon water
- 1 teaspoon cornstarch
- 2 tablespoons oyster sauce
- 1 teaspoon sugar
- 1 teaspoon black pepper
- 1 tablespoon vegetable oil
- ½ onion, thinly sliced

Directions

- **Step 1**

  Stir together 1 teaspoon vegetable oil, 1 teaspoon oyster sauce, and 1/2 teaspoon cornstarch in a bowl. Add beef and toss to coat. Marinate in the refrigerator 30 to 45 minutes. Remove from the refrigerator 10 minutes before cooking.

- **Step 2**

  Stir together water, 1 teaspoon cornstarch, 2 tablespoons oyster sauce, and pepper in a small bowl; set aside. Heat 1 tablespoon vegetable oil in a large skillet over high heat. Stir in onion, and cook until it beings to brown on the edges, about 1 minute. Add the beef, and continue cooking and stirring until the beef is just slightly pink, about 5 minutes. Pour in the sauce; cook and stir until the sauce has thickened and turned translucent, about 1 minute more.

Nutrition Facts
Per Serving:

202.2 calories; protein 12.9g 26% DV; carbohydrates 3.8g 1% DV; fat 14.8g 23% DV; cholesterol 43.2mg 14% DV; sodium 94.3mg 4% DV.

Breakfast Fried Brown Rice

Prep: 5 mins **Cook:** 10 mins **Total:** 15 mins **Servings:** 4 **Yield:** 4 cups

Ingredients

- 3 tablespoons peanut oil, divided, or more as needed
- ½ onion, chopped
- 2 large eggs large eggs
- 1 cup diced fully cooked ham
- 2 tablespoons butter
- 3 cups cooked brown rice
- 1 pinch kosher salt and freshly ground black pepper to taste
- ½ cup shredded Cheddar cheese

Directions

- **Step 1**

  Preheat a wok or skillet on high heat for 1 minute.

- **Step 2**

  Coat wok thoroughly with 2 tablespoons peanut oil; reduce heat to medium. Cook and stir onion until beginning to soften, about 3 minutes.

- **Step 3**

  Crack eggs directly into the wok. Stir quickly to scramble until eggs begin to set but are still fluid, about 1 1/2 minutes.

- **Step 4**

  Stir ham into the wok and cook just until warmed through, about 1 minute.

- **Step 5**

  Stir butter and remaining 1 tablespoon of peanut oil into the wok; let warm for 10 seconds. Add rice and stir constantly for 3 to 4 minutes, adding more oil if rice begins to stick.

- **Step 6**

  Season fried rice with salt and pepper; top with Cheddar cheese.

Cook's Notes:

Ensure your stir-fry is properly worked over the "hot spot" in your wok. Do this by flipping and stirring repeatedly, moving the bottom of the mixture to the top. If rice sticks to the wok, add a light amount of oil to help keep it moving.

Its important not to add to the serving size too much because of the limited amount of "hot spot" in your wok.

For more flavor, add a tablespoon of oyster sauce and a tablespoon of soy sauce. To clean out the fridge, substitute ham with yesterday's meat leftovers. To be more traditional, add frozen peas with the meat.

Nutrition Facts

Per Serving:

491.3 calories; protein 16.7g 33% DV; carbohydrates 37.4g 12% DV; fat 30.5g 47% DV; cholesterol 142mg 47% DV; sodium 699.6mg 28% DV.

Stir-Fried Tofu with Cashews

Prep: 10 mins **Cook:** 10 mins **Additional:** 10 mins **Total:** 30 mins **Servings:** 4 **Yield:** 4 servings

Ingredients
- ½ (12 ounce) package extra-firm tofu, sliced
- 2 tablespoons whiskey
- 1 tablespoon fish sauce
- 1 tablespoon light soy sauce
- 1 tablespoon black soy sauce
- 1 tablespoon oyster sauce
- 2 tablespoons vegetable oil, or to taste
- 1 cup unsalted raw cashews
- 5 cloves garlic, chopped
- 1 onion, julienned
- 3 tablespoons palm sugar
- 2 peppers fresh red chile peppers, sliced
- 3 tablespoons water
- 4 eaches green onions, sliced

Directions
- **Step 1**

  Combine tofu, whiskey, fish sauce, light soy sauce, black soy sauce, and oyster sauce in a bowl and marinate for 10 minutes.

- **Step 2**

  Meanwhile, heat oil in a wok over medium heat and fry cashews until browned, 3 to 5 minutes. Transfer cashews to a bowl and pour out oil.

- **Step 3**

  Add garlic to the wok and stir-fry for 1 minute. Stir in tofu and onion and stir-fry for 1 minute. Add palm sugar and chile peppers. Continue cooking for 2 more minutes. Add water and stir until well mixed. Remove from heat. Sprinkle the cashews and green onions on top.

Cook's Note:

Substitute sherry for the whiskey if preferred.

Nutrition Facts

Per Serving:

389.8 calories; protein 12.3g 25% DV; carbohydrates 31.2g 10% DV; fat 24.4g 38% DV; cholesterolmg; sodium 678.5mg 27% DV.

Mild Thai Beef with a Tangerine Sauce

Prep: 20 mins **Cook:** 25 mins **Total:** 45 mins **Servings:** 4 **Yield:** 4 servings

Ingredients
- 1 (8 ounce) package dry Chinese noodles
- ¼ cup hoisin sauce
- ¼ cup dry sherry
- 1 teaspoon tangerine zest
- ¼ teaspoon ground ginger
- 4 teaspoons vegetable oil
- 1 pound flank beef steak, cut diagonally into 2 inch strips
- 2 teaspoons vegetable oil
- ½ small butternut squash - peeled, seeded, and thinly sliced
- 1 cup sliced fresh mushrooms
- 1 large red onion, cut into 2 inch strips
- 3 cups cabbage, thinly sliced
- 1 tangerine, sectioned and seeded

Directions

- **Step 1**
  Fill a large pot with lightly salted water and bring to a rolling boil over high heat. Once the water is boiling, stir in the noodles, and return to a boil. Cook the pasta uncovered, stirring occasionally, until the pasta has cooked through, but is still firm to the bite, about 5 minutes. Drain, rinse, and set aside.

- **Step 2**
  Whisk together the hoisin sauce, sherry, tangerine zest, and ground ginger in a small bowl.

- **Step 3**
  Heat 2 teaspoons vegetable oil in a large wok or skillet over high heat. Add one half of the beef slices to the pan; cook, stirring constantly, until the meat is nicely browned, 2 to 3 minutes. Remove meat to a platter with a slotted spoon. Repeat with the remaining beef.

- **Step 4**
  Heat the remaining 2 teaspoons of oil in the pan. Stir in the butternut squash, mushrooms, and onion. Cook, stirring constantly, until vegetables are crisp-tender and slightly brown on the edges, 5 to 7 minutes. Add the cabbage, and cook and stir until slightly wilted, about 2 additional minutes.

- **Step 5**
  Reduce the heat to medium. Stir the cooked beef, tangerine sections, and hoisin mixture into the vegetables. Cook until heated through, 2 to 3 minutes. Serve over Chinese noodles.

Cook's Notes
If desired, garnish with flaked, unsweetened coconut and additional tangerine sections.

Beef broth can be substituted for the sherry.

Nutrition Facts

Per Serving:

505.7 calories; protein 23.9g 48% DV; carbohydrates 78.5g 25% DV; fat 13.6g 21% DV; cholesterol 25.7mg 9% DV; sodium 392.4mg 16% DV.

Easy Vegan Red Curry with Tofu and Vegetables

Prep: 20 mins **Cook:** 9 mins **Additional:** 20 mins **Total:** 49 mins **Servings:** 4 **Yield:** 4 servings

Ingredients

- 1 (12 ounce) package firm tofu, cubed
- 3 tablespoons light soy sauce, or more to taste
- 1 (14 ounce) can coconut milk
- 1 tablespoon Thai red curry paste, or more to taste
- 8 ounces broccoli florets
- 1 (4 ounce) package sliced fresh mushrooms
- 1 leek, cut lengthwise, washed, trimmed, and sliced thin
- 1 carrot, cut into matchsticks
- 1 squeeze lemon juice, or to taste
- 1 pinch white sugar

Directions

- **Step 1**

Combine tofu and 3 tablespoons soy sauce in a small bowl and marinate for about 20 minutes.

- **Step 2**

Remove the solid top layer of coconut cream from the coconut milk can and heat in a wok over medium heat. Add curry paste and stir-fry for 2 minutes. Add tofu, broccoli, mushrooms, leek, and carrot and stir-fry for 2 minutes. Pour in remaining coconut milk and simmer until vegetables are soft, about 5 minutes. Season with soy sauce, lemon juice, and sugar.

Cook's Notes:

I have used bell peppers, leek, chard, carrots, cauliflower, green onions, broccoli, cabbage, zucchini, and mushrooms in this recipe before, but really, any vegetable will work.

If you don't have a wok, you can also use a deep skillet.

Nutrition Facts

Per Serving:

306.3 calories; protein 12.2g 24% DV; carbohydrates 13.7g 4% DV; fat 25.3g 39% DV; cholesterolmg; sodium 518.3mg 21% DV.

Batagor Bandung (Indonesian Fried Tofu)

Prep: 35 mins **Cook:** 30 mins **Total:** 1 hr 5 mins **Servings:** 8 **Yield:** 8 servings

Ingredients

- 4 (8 ounce) containers tofu
- ½ cup prawns - peeled, deveined, and minced
- 1 egg, lightly beaten
- 1 ½ ounces ground chicken
- 1 green onion, chopped
- 2 teaspoons cornstarch
- 1 teaspoon sesame oil
- 1 pinch salt and ground white pepper to taste

Batter:

- 1 egg
- 6 tablespoons all-purpose flour
- 2 tablespoons cold water, or as needed
- Sauce:
- ⅓ cup water
- ¼ cup coarsely chopped dry roasted peanuts
- 1 fresh red chile pepper, finely chopped
- 2 cloves garlic, minced
- 2 teaspoons white vinegar
- 1 teaspoon white sugar
- 1 teaspoon salt
- 1 quart oil for frying

Directions

- **Step 1**

  Slice each tofu square diagonally to make 8 triangles. Make a cut into the base of each tofu triangle and scoop out enough of tofu to create a pocket.

- **Step 2**

  Combine scooped-out tofu pieces, prawns, egg, ground chicken, green onion, cornstarch, sesame oil, salt, and pepper in a bowl for the filling. Carefully stuff filling back into the tofu triangles; the filling will bulge out.

- **Step 3**

  Place a steamer insert into a saucepan and fill with water to just below the bottom of the steamer. Bring water to a boil. Add stuffed tofu triangles, cover, and steam for 20 minutes.

- **Step 4**

Meanwhile, make the batter. Mix egg and flour in a bowl. Whisk in enough water to give batter a medium-thin consistency.

- **Step 5**

Combine water, peanuts, red chile pepper, garlic, vinegar, salt, and sugar in a bowl. Stir until salt and sugar have dissolved and set sauce aside.

- **Step 6**

Remove cooked tofu triangles from the steamer.

- **Step 7**

Heat oil in a wok until hot. Dip triangles into the batter and slowly lower into the hot oil. Fry in batches until golden brown and the batter is cooked through, about 5 minutes. Drain on paper towels. Serve hot with the peanut sauce.

Nutrition Facts

Per Serving:

273.9 calories; protein 15g 30% DV; carbohydrates 9.7g 3% DV; fat 20.7g 32% DV; cholesterol 61.5mg 21% DV; sodium 391.1mg 16% DV.

Fried Rice with Lychees (Koa Pad Lin Gee)

Prep: 15 mins **Cook:** 30 mins **Additional:** 1 hr **Total:** 1 hr 45 mins **Servings:** 4 **Yield:** 4 servings

Ingredients

- 1 cup uncooked jasmine rice
- ½ cup water
- 3 tablespoons vegetable oil
- 2 cloves garlic, minced
- 2 tablespoons chopped carrot
- 1 tablespoon chopped onion
- 3 tablespoons soy-based liquid seasoning (such as Maggi®)
- ¼ cup reduced-sodium soy sauce
- 2 tablespoons chopped green onion
- 1 tablespoon chopped cashews
- 1 teaspoon raisins
- ¼ teaspoon white sugar
- ¼ teaspoon white pepper
- 5 eaches canned lychees, drained and quartered

Directions

- **Step 1**

Bring the rice and water to a boil in a saucepan over high heat. Reduce heat to medium-low, cover, and simmer until the rice is tender, and the liquid has been absorbed, 20 to 25 minutes. Once cooked, spread the rice into a shallow dish, and refrigerate until cold, or use 1 1/2 cups leftover cooked rice.

- **Step 2**

  Heat the oil in a wok or large skillet over medium-high heat. Stir in the garlic and cook a few seconds until fragrant, then stir in the carrots and onion, and continue cooking until the onion begins to soften. Add the cold rice, and cook and stir until hot. Pour in the soy sauce, soy seasoning, green onions, cashews, raisins, salt, and white pepper. Cook and stir until hot, then stir in the quartered lychees to serve.

Nutrition Facts
Per Serving:
301.8 calories; protein 4.7g 9% DV; carbohydrates 45.5g 15% DV; fat 11.3g 17% DV; cholesterolmg; sodium 549.7mg 22% DV.

Chinese Dong'an Chicken

Prep: 30 mins **Cook:** 27 mins **Total:** 57 mins **Servings:** 4 **Yield:** 4 servings

Ingredients
- 1 (2 pound) whole chicken
- 1 tablespoon cornstarch
- 1 tablespoon cold water
- 6 tablespoons peanut oil
- 1 ½ tablespoons grated fresh ginger
- 2 teaspoons finely chopped dried chile peppers
- 3 tablespoons vinegar
- 1 ½ tablespoons rice wine
- 20 eaches Szechuan peppercorns, crushed
- 1 pinch salt to taste
- 2 eaches spring onions, chopped, or more to taste
- ⅛ teaspoon monosodium glutamate (MSG)
- 2 teaspoons sesame oil

Directions
- **Step 1**

  Place chicken in a stockpot with water to cover; bring to a boil and cook until juices run clear, at least 20 minutes. An instant-read thermometer inserted into the thickest part of the thigh near the bone should read 165 degrees F (74 degrees C). Remove chicken; set aside to cool. Reserve 1/2 cup of the cooking liquid.

- **Step 2**

Remove chicken meat from bone; cut meat into 1/2-inch by 2-inch strips. Mix cornstarch and cold water together in a small bowl. Toss meat in 1/2 of the cornstarch mixture.

- **Step 3**

  Heat peanut oil in a wok or large skillet over high heat. Add chicken mixture, ginger, and chiles; cook and stir until fragrant, 2 to 3 minutes. Add reserved cooking liquid, vinegar, rice wine, peppercorns, and salt. Return to boil; cook and stir until mixture is almost dry, about 3 minutes. Stir in spring onions, monosodium glutamate, and remaining cornstarch mixture; cook until sauce is thickened, 2 to 3 minutes more. Drizzle with sesame oil.

Cook's Note:

Substitute the ½ cup cooking liquid with ½ cup prepared chicken stock, if desired.

Nutrition Facts

Per Serving:

696.8 calories; protein 20.2g 40% DV; carbohydrates 6.5g 2% DV; fat 65g 100% DV; cholesterol 80.3mg 27% DV; sodium 130.1mg 5% DV.

Easy Chicken and Vegetable Stir-Fry

Prep: 45 mins **Cook:** 20 mins **Total:** 1 hr 5 mins **Servings:** 6 **Yield:** 6 servings

Ingredients

- 2 tablespoons vegetable oil
- 1 ½ pounds skinless, boneless chicken breasts, cut into bite-sized pieces
- 2 (8 ounce) cans sliced water chestnuts, drained
- 2 stalks celery, sliced
- 2 carrot, (7-1/2")s carrots, sliced
- ½ pound fresh green beans, cut into pieces
- ½ pound fresh mushrooms, sliced
- ½ pound fresh bean sprouts
- ½ pound fresh broccoli, cut into pieces
- ½ pound fresh green cabbage, cut into pieces
- 1 ½ cups stir-fry sauce (such as Kikkoman®)
- ½ cup minced garlic
- 7 eaches green onion stalks, cut into pieces
- 2 tablespoons sesame seeds, or to taste
- 2 tablespoons ground ginger, or to taste
- ½ teaspoon salt, or to taste

Directions

- **Step 1**

Heat oil in a large wok over high heat. Add chicken, water chestnuts, celery, carrots, green beans, mushrooms, bean sprouts, broccoli, cabbage, stir-fry sauce, garlic, green onion, sesame seeds, ground ginger, and salt. Cook, stirring often, until vegetables are tender to taste and chicken is no longer pink inside and juices run clear, 20 to 30 minutes.

Nutrition Facts

Per Serving:

424.9 calories; protein 30.8g 62% DV; carbohydrates 42.8g 14% DV; fat 15.5g 24% DV; cholesterol 64.6mg 22% DV; sodium 864.6mg 35% DV.

Bok Choy with Pine Nuts and Sesame Seeds

Prep: 10 mins **Cook:** 8 mins **Total:** 18 mins **Servings:** 4 **Yield:** 4 servings

Ingredients

- 1 teaspoon sesame oil
- 1 red onion, finely sliced
- 2 cloves garlic, finely sliced
- 1 pound baby bok choy, trimmed
- 1 tablespoon light soy sauce
- 2 teaspoons fish sauce
- 1 tablespoon toasted pine nuts
- 2 teaspoons toasted sesame seeds
- 1 cup Thai basil

Directions

- **Step 1**

  Heat sesame oil in a wok or large skillet over low heat. Cook and stir onion and garlic until soft, about 5 minutes. Add bok choy and continue to stir-fry. Add soy sauce, fish sauce, pine nuts, toasted sesame seeds and Thai basil. Stir-fry until the green tips of the bok choy and the basil are just wilted, about 3 minutes.

Nutrition Facts

Per Serving:

64.8 calories; protein 3.5g 7% DV; carbohydrates 6.9g 2% DV; fat 3.4g 5% DV; cholesterolmg; sodium 391mg 16% DV.

Chicken, Snow Pea, and Cashew Fried Rice

Prep: 15 mins **Cook:** 8 mins **Total:** 23 mins **Servings:** 4 **Yield:** 4 servings

Ingredients

- 1 pound skinless, boneless chicken breasts, cut into thin strips

- ¼ cup teriyaki sauce, divided
- 3 tablespoons vegetable oil, divided
- 3 eaches scallions, thinly sliced
- 2 cloves garlic, minced
- 1 tablespoon minced fresh ginger root
- 8 ounces snow peas, trimmed
- ¼ cup low-sodium chicken broth
- 4 cups cooked white rice
- 3 tablespoons chopped roasted cashews

Directions

- **Step 1**

  Combine chicken and 2 tablespoons teriyaki sauce in a bowl. Heat 1 1/2 tablespoons vegetable oil in a large skillet or wok over high heat. Add chicken; cook and stir until no longer pink in the center, 3 to 5 minutes. Transfer to a separate bowl.

- **Step 2**

  Stir scallions, garlic, ginger, and remaining vegetable oil into skillet until fragrant, about 1 minute. Stir in snow peas and chicken broth; cover and cook until tender; 2 to 3 minutes.

- **Step 3**

  Stir rice, cooked chicken, and remaining teriyaki sauce into skillet; cook and stir until rice is heated through, 2 to 3 minutes. Sprinkle with cashews.

Nutrition Facts

Per Serving:

505.7 calories; protein 32g 64% DV; carbohydrates 55.3g 18% DV; fat 16.5g 25% DV; cholesterol 64.9mg 22% DV; sodium 800.4mg 32% DV.

Garlic-Mushroom Chicken Thigh Stir-Fry

Prep: 10 mins **Cook:** 10 mins **Total:** 20 mins **Servings:** 2 **Yield:** 2 servings

Ingredients

- Stir-Fry Sauce:
- ⅓ cup water
- 2 tablespoons brown sugar
- 2 tablespoons vinegar
- 1 ½ tablespoons soy sauce
- 1 ½ teaspoons sesame oil
- 1 teaspoon garlic paste
- 1 teaspoon fish sauce
- 1 teaspoon oyster sauce

- 2 teaspoons tapioca flour
- Stir-Fry Mixture:
- 1 tablespoon sesame oil
- 1 green bell pepper, sliced into strips
- 4 ounces portobello mushrooms, sliced
- 1 small onion, cut into wedges
- 8 ounces skinless, boneless chicken thighs, cut into bite-sized pieces
- 2 cloves garlic, sliced
- ½ teaspoon minced fresh ginger

Directions

- **Step 1**

Combine water, brown sugar, vinegar, soy sauce, sesame oil, garlic paste, fish sauce, and oyster sauce in a bowl. Dissolve tapioca flour in soy sauce mixture to make the sauce. Set aside.

- **Step 2**

Heat sesame oil in a large wok. Add bell pepper, mushrooms, and onion. Cook, stirring occasionally, until vegetables have softened, about 5 minutes. Add chicken and cook until chicken is no longer pink inside and juices run clear, about 5 minutes. Add sliced garlic; cook and stir until garlic is fragrant, about 1 minute. Pour in sauce. Cook and stir until sauce thickens slightly, about 5 minutes.

Nutrition Facts
Per Serving:
409.9 calories; protein 23.6g 47% DV; carbohydrates 29.2g 9% DV; fat 22g 34% DV; cholesterol 73.2mg 24% DV; sodium 1041mg 42% DV.

Fried Rice with Corned Beef, Spinach, and Eggs

Prep: 10 mins **Cook:** 15 mins **Total:** 25 mins **Servings:** 8 **Yield:** 8 servings

Ingredients

- 1 tablespoon vegetable oil
- 2 cups shredded and chopped cooked corned beef
- 4 ounces spinach, chopped
- 3 large eggs eggs, lightly whisked
- 5 cups cooked rice
- 1 teaspoon garlic powder, or to taste
- 1 pinch salt to taste

Directions

- **Step 1**

Heat vegetable oil in a wok or large skillet over medium heat. Add corned beef; cook and stir until heated through, about 3 minutes. Add spinach; cook and stir until wilted, about 2 minutes.

- **Step 2**

    Push beef and spinach to the sides of the work; pour eggs into the center; cook, stirring frequently, until eggs are scrambled, about 3 minutes. Stir in rice; cook until heated through, about 5 minutes. Season with garlic powder and salt.

Nutrition Facts

Per Serving:

295.1 calories; protein 14.2g 28% DV; carbohydrates 28.9g 9% DV; fat 13g 20% DV; cholesterol 116.8mg 39% DV; sodium 602.1mg 24% DV.

Paleo Spicy Shrimp Stir-Fry

Prep: 20 mins **Cook:** 10 mins **Additional:** 8 hrs **Total:** 8 hrs 30 mins **Servings:** 4 **Yield:** 24 shrimp

Ingredients

- ½ cup lemon juice
- 1 small onion, finely chopped
- ½ cup olive oil
- 3 cloves garlic, minced
- 1 tablespoon lemon zest
- 1 tablespoon grated ginger
- 1 teaspoon ground turmeric
- 24 eaches large shrimp, peeled and deveined
- 1 tablespoon coconut oil, or as needed

Directions

- **Step 1**

    Mix together lemon juice, onion, olive oil, garlic, lemon zest, ginger, and turmeric in a bowl. Place shrimp into marinade, cover, and refrigerate shrimp and marinade mixture overnight.

- **Step 2**

    Remove shrimp, saving the marinade. Heat a wok or skillet over medium-high heat; melt coconut oil in hot wok. Stir-fry shrimp in coconut oil until shrimp are opaque and pink, 5 to 10 minutes. Add reserved marinade and bring to a boil, stirring constantly.

Nutrition Facts

Per Serving:

387.7 calories; protein 21.1g 42% DV; carbohydrates 5.9g 2% DV; fat 31.7g 49% DV; cholesterol 191.6mg 64% DV; sodium 222.5mg 9% DV.

Corned Beef Fried Rice with Mint

Prep: 10 mins **Cook:** 10 mins **Total:** 20 mins **Servings:** 2 **Yield:** 2 servings

Ingredients
- 1 tablespoon olive oil
- 2 cups cooked white rice
- 1 teaspoon chicken soup base (such as Better than Bouillon®)
- 6 ounces cooked corned beef, thinly sliced
- 1 egg, beaten
- 6 sprig (blank)s fresh spearmint leaves, cut into thin strips

Directions
- **Step 1**

  Heat olive oil in a wok over medium-high heat.
- **Step 2**

  Cook and stir rice and chicken paste in hot oil until combined, about 2 minutes.
- **Step 3**

  Stir corned beef into rice mixture until rice begins to brown, 2 to 4 minutes.
- **Step 4**

  Remove the wok from heat and clear a hole in the center of the rice to cook egg.
- **Step 5**

  Pour the beaten egg into center of the rice. Tilt the wok around to spread the egg into the rice, allowing the residual heat to completely cook the egg.
- **Step 6**

  Portion the fried rice into 2 bowls and top with fresh mint.

Nutrition Facts

Per Serving:

429.7 calories; protein 24.4g 49% DV; carbohydrates 46.5g 15% DV; fat 15.7g 24% DV; cholesterol 148.9mg 50% DV; sodium 1569.2mg 63% DV.

Thai Pad Thai Noodles

Prep: 10 mins **Cook:** 15 mins **Additional:** 20 mins **Total:** 45 mins **Servings:** 4 **Yield:** 4 servings

Ingredients
- 3 cups water
- 1 (8 ounce) package wide rice noodles
- 2 ½ tablespoons vegetable oil
- 2 cloves garlic, smashed
- 1 (4 ounce) boneless pork chop, cut into small pieces
- 1 cup bean sprouts

- 3 tablespoons dried small shrimp
- 2 ½ tablespoons palm sugar
- 2 tablespoons fish sauce
- 1 tablespoon soy sauce
- 1 tablespoon lime juice
- 2 tablespoons chopped salted radish
- ¼ cup unsalted roasted peanuts, chopped
- ¼ cup chopped fresh cilantro for garnish

Directions
- **Step 1**

  Bring water to a boil in a pot.
- **Step 2**

  Place rice noodles in a large bowl. Pour boiling water over noodles and allow to soak until softened, about 20 minutes. Drain.
- **Step 3**

  Heat vegetable oil in a wok over medium heat.
- **Step 4**

  Cook and stir garlic and pork in hot oil until pork is no longer pink in the center, about 5 minutes.
- **Step 5**

  Stir in soaked rice noodles, bean sprouts, dried shrimp, palm sugar, fish sauce, soy sauce, and lime juice, stirring until palm sugar has dissolved. Cook until noodles are heated through, 3 to 4 minutes.
- **Step 6**

  Stir in salted radish until combined.
- **Step 7**

  Lightly toss peanuts and noodle mixture together until combined Transfer to a platter. Garnish with cilantro.

Nutrition Facts
Per Serving:

374.1 calories; protein 9.7g 19% DV; carbohydrates 50g 16% DV; fat 15.3g 24% DV; cholesterol 17.4mg 6% DV; sodium 908.4mg 36% DV.

Panang Curry with Chicken

Prep: 15 mins **Cook:** 20 mins **Total:** 35 mins **Servings:** 4 **Yield:** 4 servings

Ingredients

- 5 tablespoons Panang curry paste
- 2 tablespoons cooking oil
- 4 cups coconut milk
- ⅔ pound skinless, boneless chicken breast, cubed
- 2 tablespoons palm sugar
- 2 tablespoons fish sauce, or to taste
- 6 leaf (blank)s kaffir lime leaves, torn
- 2 peppers fresh red chile peppers, sliced
- ¼ cup fresh Thai basil leaves

Directions

- **Step 1**

Fry the curry paste in the oil in a large skillet or wok over medium heat until fragrant. Stir the coconut milk into the curry paste and bring to a boil. Add the chicken; cook and stir until the chicken is nearly cooked through, 10 to 15 minutes. Stir the palm sugar, fish sauce, and lime leaves into the mixture; simmer together for 5 minutes. Taste and adjust the saltiness by adding more fish sauce if necessary. Garnish with sliced red chile peppers and Thai basil leaves to serve.

Nutrition Facts

Per Serving:

596 calories; protein 22.3g 45% DV; carbohydrates 18.5g 6% DV; fat 51.2g 79% DV; cholesterol 46mg 15% DV; sodium 980.5mg 39% DV.

Thai Spicy Basil Chicken Fried Rice

Prep: 30 mins **Cook:** 10 mins **Total:** 40 mins **Servings:** 6 **Yield:** 6 servings

Ingredients

- 3 tablespoons oyster sauce
- 2 tablespoons fish sauce
- 1 teaspoon white sugar
- ½ cup peanut oil for frying
- 4 cups cooked jasmine rice, chilled
- 6 large cloves garlic clove, crushed
- 2 peppers serrano peppers, crushed
- 1 pound boneless, skinless chicken breast, cut into thin strips
- 1 red pepper, seeded and thinly sliced
- 1 onion, thinly sliced
- 2 cups sweet Thai basil
- 1 cucumber, sliced

- ½ cup cilantro sprigs

Directions

- **Step 1**

  Whisk together the oyster sauce, fish sauce, and sugar in a bowl.

- **Step 2**

  Heat the oil in a wok over medium-high heat until the oil begins to smoke. Add the garlic and serrano peppers, stirring quickly. Stir in the chicken, bell pepper, onion and oyster sauce mixture; cook until the chicken is no longer pink. Raise heat to high and stir in the chilled rice; stir quickly until the sauce is blended with the rice. Use the back of a spoon to break up any rice sticking together.

- **Step 3**

  Remove from heat and mix in the basil leaves. Garnish with sliced cucumber and cilantro as desired.

Nutrition Facts

Per Serving:

794.1 calories; protein 29.1g 58% DV; carbohydrates 116.4g 38% DV; fat 22.1g 34% DV; cholesterol 46.1mg 15% DV; sodium 469.1mg 19% DV.

Easy Pineapple Chicken

Prep: 15 mins **Cook:** 25 mins **Total:** 40 mins **Servings:** 4 **Yield:** 4 servings

Ingredients

- 3 tablespoons soy sauce
- 3 tablespoons olive oil, divided
- ½ teaspoon paprika
- 1 pinch salt to taste
- 1 pound boneless, skinless chicken breast, cut into strips
- 1 red bell pepper, cubed
- 1 bunch scallions, trimmed and sliced into 1/2-inch lengths
- 1 (12 ounce) can pineapple chunks, drained and juice reserved
- 1 tablespoon cornstarch

Directions

- **Step 1**

  Combine soy sauce, 2 tablespoons olive oil, paprika, and salt in a bowl. Add chicken strips and let marinate while preparing the remaining ingredients.

- **Step 2**

  Heat the remaining 1 tablespoon of olive oil in a wok. Add bell pepper and stir-fry for 3 minutes. Add scallions and cook for 2 more minutes. Remove chicken from marinade and add to the wok; discard marinade. Cook, stirring occasionally, until chicken is cooked through and no longer pink in the centre, 10 to 15 minutes.

- **Step 3**

  Combine pineapple juice and cornstarch in a bowl; mix together. Add pineapple chunks to the skillet and cook for 2 to 3 minutes. Pour in pineapple juice mixture and bring to a boil. Simmer until sauce has thickened, about 3 minutes.

Cook's Note:

You can also use a large skillet instead of a wok.

Nutrition Facts

Per Serving:

307.3 calories; protein 26.1g 52% DV; carbohydrates 22g 7% DV; fat 13.1g 20% DV; cholesterol 64.6mg 22% DV; sodium 782.9mg 31% DV.

Myra's Basil Chicken Stir Fry

Prep: 10 mins **Cook:** 15 mins **Additional:** 30 mins **Total:** 55 mins **Servings:** 6 **Yield:** 6 servings

Ingredients

- 1 tablespoon soy sauce
- 2 tablespoons water
- 1 tablespoon white sugar
- 2 pounds skinless, boneless chicken breast halves, cut into small pieces
- 1 tablespoon vegetable oil
- 5 eaches green onions, sliced
- 3 cloves garlic, chopped
- 3 tablespoons vegetable oil
- 2 (6 ounce) bags fresh baby spinach leaves
- 1 cup thinly sliced fresh basil

Directions

- **Step 1**

  Combine soy sauce, water, and sugar in a bowl.

- **Step 2**

  Marinate chicken in soy sauce mixture for 30 minutes.

- **Step 3**

  Heat 1 tablespoon oil in a large skillet or wok over medium heat.

- **Step 4**

  Cook and stir green onions in oil for 1 minute. Add garlic and cook and stir for 1 minute. Transfer to a small bowl.

- **Step 5**

Pour 3 tablespoons oil into the skillet. Cook and stir chicken and marinade until chicken is no longer pink in the center and juices run clear, about 5 minutes.

- **Step 6**

   Add spinach leaves to chicken. Cover for 4 minutes stirring occasionally.

- **Step 7**

   Stir green onion mixture into chicken and spinach; cook to reheat onions, 1 to 2 minutes.

- **Step 8**

   Stir in basil and cook until heated, 1 to 2 minutes. Serve!

Nutrition Facts

Per Serving:

277.9 calories; protein 33.8g 68% DV; carbohydrates 5.9g 2% DV; fat 13g 20% DV; cholesterol 86.1mg 29% DV; sodium 272.6mg 11% DV.

Crispy Shrimp Tempura

Prep: 20 mins **Cook:** 15 mins **Total:** 35 mins **Servings:** 6 **Yield:** 6 servings

Ingredients

- 1 cup all-purpose flour
- 2 tablespoons cornstarch
- 1 pinch salt
- 1 cup water
- 1 egg yolk
- 2 large egg whites egg whites, lightly beaten
- 1 pound medium shrimp, peeled and deveined, tails left on
- 2 cups vegetable oil for frying

Directions

- **Step 1**

   Heat oil in a deep-fryer to 375 degrees F (190 degrees C).

- **Step 2**

   Whisk flour, cornstarch, and salt in a large bowl. Make a depression in the center of the flour. Stir in the water and egg yolk. Mix just until moistened; batter will be lumpy. Stir in egg whites.

- **Step 3**

   One at a time, dip shrimp into the batter to coat. Do not batter tails. Carefully place a few shrimp at a time into the hot oil. Fry until golden brown, about 1 1/2 minutes. Drain on paper towels.

Nutrition Facts

Per Serving:

891.2 calories; protein 16.4g 33% DV; carbohydrates 25.3g 8% DV; fat 81.5g 125% DV; cholesterol 138.6mg 46% DV; sodium 224.6mg 9% DV.

Beef Lo Mein

Prep: 15 mins **Cook:** 25 mins **Total:** 40 mins **Servings:** 4 **Yield:** 4 servings

Ingredients

- 1 (8 ounce) package spaghetti
- 1 teaspoon dark sesame oil
- 1 tablespoon peanut oil
- 4 cloves garlic, minced
- 1 tablespoon minced fresh ginger root
- 4 cups mixed vegetables
- 1 pound flank steak, thinly sliced
- 3 tablespoons reduced-sodium soy sauce
- 2 tablespoons brown sugar
- 1 tablespoon oyster sauce
- 1 tablespoon Asian chile paste with garlic

Directions

- **Step 1**

  Bring a large pot of lightly salted water to a boil. Cook spaghetti in the boiling water until cooked through but firm to the bite, about 12 minutes; drain and transfer to a large bowl. Drizzle sesame oil over the spaghetti; toss to coat. Place a plate atop the bowl to keep the noodles warm.

- **Step 2**

  Heat peanut oil in a wok or large skillet over medium-high heat. Cook and stir garlic and ginger in hot oil until fragrant, about 30 seconds. Add mixed vegetables to the skillet; cook and stir until slightly tender, about 3 minutes. Stir flank steak into the vegetable mixture; cook and stir until the beef is cooked through, about 5 minutes.

- **Step 3**

  Mix soy sauce, brown sugar, oyster sauce, and chile paste together in a small bowl; pour over the spaghetti. Dump spaghetti and sauce mixture into the wok with the vegetables and steak; cook and stir until the spaghetti is hot, 2 to 3 minutes.

Cook's Note:

I added a small package of sliced mushrooms, a shredded broccoli, carrots, cabbage mix (coleslaw mix) and snap peas, but you can pretty much add whatever veggies you like. About 4 to 5 cups of veggies is a good amount.

Nutrition Facts
Per Serving:

519.3 calories; protein 26.3g 53% DV; carbohydrates 72.8g 24% DV; fat 15g 23% DV; cholesterol 35.6mg 12% DV; sodium 573.5mg 23% DV.

Mushroom Pepper Steak

Total Time Prep: 15 min. + marinating Cook: 15 min. Makes 4 servings

Ingredients

- 6 tablespoons reduced-sodium soy sauce, divided
- 1/8 teaspoon pepper
- 1 pound beef top sirloin steak, cut into thin strips
- 1 tablespoon cornstarch
- 1/2 cup reduced-sodium beef broth
- 1 garlic clove, minced
- 1/2 teaspoon minced fresh gingerroot
- 3 teaspoons canola oil, divided
- 1 cup julienned sweet red pepper
- 1 cup julienned green pepper
- 2 cups sliced fresh mushrooms
- 2 medium tomatoes, cut into wedges
- 6 green onions, sliced
- Hot cooked rice, optional

Directions

- In a shallow bowl, combine 3 tablespoons soy sauce and pepper; add beef. Turn to coat; cover and refrigerate 30-60 minutes. In a small bowl, combine the cornstarch, broth and remaining soy sauce until smooth; set aside.
- Drain beef, discarding marinade. In a <u>large nonstick skillet</u> or wok, stir-fry the garlic and ginger in 2 teaspoons oil for 1 minute. Add the beef; stir-fry 4-6 minutes or until no longer pink. Remove beef and keep warm.
- Stir-fry the peppers in remaining oil for 1 minute. Add mushrooms; stir-fry 2 minutes longer or until peppers are crisp-tender. Stir broth mixture and add to vegetable mixture. Bring to a boil; cook and stir for 2 minutes or until thickened. Return beef to pan; add tomatoes and onions. Cook for 2 minutes or until heated through. Serve over rice if desired.

Nutrition Facts

1-1/4 cups beef mixture: 241 calories, 10g fat (3g saturated fat), 64mg cholesterol, 841mg sodium, 13g carbohydrate (5g sugars, 3g fiber), 25g protein. Diabetic exchanges: 3 lean meat, 2 vegetable, 1 fat.

Pineapple Fried Rice II

Prep: 15 mins **Cook:** 30 mins **Additional:** 20 mins **Total:** 1 hr 5 mins **Servings:** 4 **Yield:** 4 servings

Ingredients
- 1 cup uncooked white rice
- 2 cups water
- 2 tablespoons sesame oil
- 3 eaches green onions, thinly sliced including tops
- 1 cup diced ham
- ½ cup peas
- 1 (8 ounce) can pineapple chunks, drained
- 1 egg, beaten
- 1 tablespoon white sugar
- 1 teaspoon salt
- ½ teaspoon white pepper
- ½ teaspoon garlic powder
- ¼ cup soy sauce

Directions
- **Step 1**
  Bring the rice and water to a boil in a saucepan over high heat. Reduce heat to medium-low, cover, and simmer until the rice is tender, and the liquid has been absorbed, 20 to 25 minutes. Spread cooked rice out on a rimmed baking sheet and refrigerate until cooled, about 20 minutes.
- **Step 2**
  Heat sesame oil in a large skillet or wok over medium-high heat. Cook and stir the green onions, ham, and peas in the hot oil until onions have softened, about 2 minutes. Stir the pineapple chunks into the wok; cook until pineapple begins to darken, about 2 minute. Push ingredients to the side of the wok, and pour beaten egg in the center. Cook until egg begins to set, about 30 seconds. Stir together all contents of the wok.
- **Step 3**
  Mix the cooled rice, sugar, salt, white pepper, and garlic powder into the wok; stir constantly to keep from sticking. Cook until heated through, about 3 minutes. Sprinkle the rice with the soy sauce, and stir to combine.

Cook's Note:

Vegetable oil can be substituted for sesame oil when stir-frying. To keep rice from sticking, make sure wok is very hot and well oiled.

Nutrition Facts

Per Serving:

374.1 calories; protein 12.8g 26% DV; carbohydrates 55.4g 18% DV; fat 11.3g 17% DV; cholesterol 60.2mg 20% DV; sodium 2000.7mg 80% DV.

Caribbean Jerk Stir-Fry

Prep: 15 mins **Cook:** 20 mins **Total:** 35 mins **Servings:** 2 **Yield:** 2 servings

Ingredients

- 1 tablespoon vegetable oil
- 1 green bell pepper, seeded and cubed
- 1 red bell pepper, seeded and cubed
- ¼ cup sliced sweet onions
- ¾ pound skinless, boneless chicken breast, cut into strips
- 2 ½ teaspoons Caribbean jerk seasoning
- ½ cup plum sauce
- 1 tablespoon soy sauce
- ¼ cup chopped roasted peanuts

Directions

- **Step 1**

Heat the oil in a large skillet over medium-high heat. Cook and stir the bell pepper and onion in the oil until slightly tender, 5 to 7 minutes. Remove pepper and onion from the skillet and set aside. Add the chicken to the skillet; season with jerk seasoning; cook and stir chicken until no longer pink inside. Pour the plum sauce in with the chicken; add the bell peppers and onions; toss to combine. Cook until the peppers and onions are heated completely, 3 to 5 minutes. Sprinkle with soy sauce and chopped peanuts to serve.

Nutrition Facts

Per Serving:

548.8 calories; protein 44.3g 89% DV; carbohydrates 41g 13% DV; fat 21.4g 33% DV; cholesterol 103.7mg 35% DV; sodium 1620.6mg 65% DV.

Erika's Ginger Beef

Prep: 20 mins **Cook:** 25 mins **Total:** 45 mins **Servings:** 6 **Yield:** 6 servings

Ingredients

- 1 ½ pounds beef top round steak, cut into thin slices
- 2 large eggs eggs, beaten
- 1 cup cornstarch
- ½ cup water
- 1 cup oil for frying, or as needed
- 1 tablespoon sesame oil
- 2 carrot, (7-1/2")s carrots, cut into matchstick-size pieces
- 1 green onion, chopped
- 5 tablespoons minced fresh ginger root
- 5 cloves garlic, chopped

- ¼ cup soy sauce
- 2 tablespoons white vinegar
- ½ cup white sugar
- ¼ teaspoon red pepper flakes
- 1 tablespoon sesame seeds, or as needed

Directions

- **Step 1**

  Stir beef and eggs together in a bowl. Whisk cornstarch and water together; stir into beef mixture.

- **Step 2**

  Pour oil 2 to 3 inches deep in a wok; heat to 350 degrees F (175 degrees C). Cook beef strips in oil, working in batches, until brown and crisp, about 4 minutes; remove to drain and keep warm. Repeat with remaining beef.

- **Step 3**

  Heat sesame oil in a large nonstick skillet over medium high heat; stir in carrots, green onion, ginger, and garlic. Cook and stir until vegetables begin to soften, about 5 minutes. Stir soy sauce, white vinegar, sugar, and red pepper flakes into vegetable mixture; bring to a boil. Stir beef strips into vegetables; sprinkle with sesame seeds.

Cook's Note:

It is easier to slice beef thinly when it is partially frozen.

Red bell peppers are nice in this dish, too. Add more carrot and green onion if you like.

Nutrition Facts

Per Serving:

414.8 calories; protein 26.7g 53% DV; carbohydrates 41.6g 13% DV; fat 15.3g 24% DV; cholesterol 122.4mg 41% DV; sodium 675.5mg 27% DV.

Super Simple Spicy Fried Tofu

Prep: 10 mins **Cook:** 10 mins **Total:** 20 mins **Servings:** 4 **Yield:** 4 servings

Ingredients

- 1 (10 ounce) package fried tofu
- 1 tablespoon sesame oil
- 1 onion, chopped
- 1 medium red bell pepper, chopped
- 2 tablespoons brown sugar
- 1 tablespoon soy sauce
- 2 teaspoons chili-garlic sauce, or more to taste
- 2 eaches green onions, chopped

Directions

- **Step 1**

  Drain tofu, rinse, and pat dry. Cut into squares.

- **Step 2**

  Heat sesame oil in a wok over medium heat. Add onion and cook for 2 minutes. Add red pepper and stir-fry for 2 minutes. Stir in tofu and cook for 2 minutes. Stir in brown sugar, soy sauce, and chili-garlic sauce. Mix together and cook for 3 minutes. Adjust seasoning to taste. Sprinkle with green onions before serving.

Cook's Notes:

Substitute tamari for soy sauce if desired.

Substitute palm sugar for brown sugar if desired.

Nutrition Facts

Per Serving:

274 calories; protein 13.2g 26% DV; carbohydrates 19.6g 6% DV; fat 17.8g 27% DV; cholesterolmg; sodium 355.6mg 14% DV.

Green Curry with Sweet Potato and Aubergine (Eggplant)

Prep: 20 mins **Cook:** 27 mins **Total:** 47 mins **Servings:** 5 **Yield:** 5 servings

Ingredients

- 1 tablespoon vegetable oil
- 1 onion, chopped
- 1 tablespoon green curry paste, or more to taste
- 1 eggplant, quartered and sliced
- 1 (14 ounce) can coconut milk
- 1 cup vegetable stock
- 1 sweet potato, peeled and sliced
- 6 leaf (blank)s kaffir lime leaves
- 2 tablespoons lime juice
- 2 teaspoons lime zest
- 2 teaspoons soft brown sugar
- 1 pinch salt
- 1 shredded kaffir lime leaf for garnish
- 1 sprig chopped fresh cilantro for garnish

Directions

- **Step 1**

Heat oil in a large wok or skillet over medium heat. Add onion and curry paste; cook and stir until fragrant, about 3 minutes. Stir in eggplant; cook until softened, 4 to 5 minutes.

- **Step 2**
Pour coconut milk and vegetable stock onto the eggplant mixture. Bring to a boil; reduce heat and simmer until heated through, about 5 minutes. Stir in sweet potato and lime leaves; cook and stir until vegetables are tender, about 10 minutes. Mix in lime juice, lime zest, and brown sugar; stir until combined. Season with salt; garnish with shredded lime leaf and cilantro.

Nutrition Facts
Per Serving:
276.6 calories; protein 4g 8% DV; carbohydrates 25.3g 8% DV; fat 19.8g 31% DV; cholesterolmg; sodium 188.8mg 8% DV.

China Sun Chicken

Prep: 25 mins **Cook:** 15 mins **Total:** 40 mins **Servings:** 3 **Yield:** 3 servings

Ingredients
- 2 tablespoons vegetable oil
- 1 pound skinless, boneless chicken breast halves - cut into 1/2 inch pieces
- 2 medium (blank)s carrots, julienned
- 2 cloves garlic, pressed
- 1 teaspoon ground ginger
- 4 eaches shallots, chopped
- 1 bell pepper, slivered
- 1 (20 ounce) can pineapple chunks in natural juice, liquid drained and reserved
- ½ cup water
- 2 tablespoons soy sauce
- 1 tablespoon cornstarch
- 1 teaspoon white vinegar
- ½ teaspoon red pepper flakes

Directions
- **Step 1**
Heat the oil in a wok or large skillet over medium-high heat; cook the chicken and carrots in the hot oil until the chicken is no longer pink in the center and the carrots are tender, about 5 minutes. Stir in the garlic and ginger; cook another 1 minute. Add the shallots and bell pepper; cook another 1 minute.
- **Step 2**
Whisk together 3 tablespoons of the reserved liquid from the canned pineapple chunks along with the pineapple chunks, the water, soy sauce, cornstarch, vinegar, and pepper flakes; stir into the chicken and vegetable mixture and bring to a boil, stirring until the sauce thickens.

Nutrition Facts

Per Serving:

476.9 calories; protein 38g 76% DV; carbohydrates 51.4g 17% DV; fat 14.4g 22% DV; cholesterol 92.2mg 31% DV; sodium 722.6mg 29% DV.

Makato's Bacon Fried Rice

Prep: 15 mins **Cook:** 10 mins **Total:** 25 mins **Servings:** 4 **Yield:** 4 servings

Ingredients

- ½ pound bacon, sliced into small pieces
- 2 tablespoons soy sauce
- 2 medium (4-1/8" long)s green onions, chopped
- ¼ teaspoon sea salt
- 2 cups steamed white rice

Directions

- **Step 1**

Place bacon in a wok or large skillet and cook over medium heat, stirring occasionally, until starting to brown, about 5 minutes. Pour in soy sauce and scrape up any brown bits from the bottom of the wok. Add green onions and salt; cook until wilted, 30 seconds to 1 minute. Add rice; cook, stirring frequently, until heated through, 3 to 4 minutes.

Nutrition Facts

Per Serving:

209.4 calories; protein 9.6g 19% DV; carbohydrates 23.7g 8% DV; fat 8g 12% DV; cholesterol 20.4mg 7% DV; sodium 990.3mg 40% DV.

Spicy Ma Po Tofu

Prep: 15 mins **Cook:** 9 mins **Additional:** 1 min **Total:** 25 mins **Servings:** 4 **Yield:** 4 servings

Ingredients

- 1 (16 ounce) package soft tofu, cut into 1/3-inch cubes
- 1 tablespoon cornstarch
- 1 tablespoon water, or as needed
- 6 ½ tablespoons vegetable oil
- 2 eaches spring onions, roughly chopped
- 1 (3/4 inch thick) slice fresh ginger, chopped
- 2 teaspoons Sichuan peppercorns
- 1 clove garlic, minced

- 5 ounces ground pork
- 1 tablespoon doubanjiang (spicy broad bean paste)
- 2 teaspoons rice wine
- 1 teaspoon soy sauce
- 1 teaspoon salt, or to taste

Directions
- **Step 1**

    Place tofu in a bowl and cover with boiling water. Let sit for 1 minute; drain.
- **Step 2**

    Mix water and cornstarch together in a bowl to make a runny paste.
- **Step 3**

    Heat oil in a wok or large skillet over medium heat. Cook and stir spring onions, ginger, peppercorns, and garlic until fragrant, about 1 minute. Stir in ground pork, doubanjiang paste, rice wine, and soy sauce; cook, stirring frequently, until pork is browned, about 5 minutes.
- **Step 4**

    Stir drained tofu into the wok or skillet. Cook and stir until coated with sauce, about 2 minutes. Season with salt. Pour in cornstarch paste and mix well until sauce thickens, about 1 minute.

Cook's Note:

Doubanjiang is a spicy paste made from fermented broad beans. You can find it in Asian or specialty shops, or online.

Nutrition Facts

Per Serving:

357.9 calories; protein 14.7g 29% DV; carbohydrates 6.3g 2% DV; fat 31.4g 48% DV; cholesterol 22.8mg 8% DV; sodium 917.4mg 37% DV.

Ultimate Pad Thai

Prep: 35 mins **Cook:** 25 mins **Additional:** 15 mins **Total:** 1 hr 15 mins **Servings:** 6 **Yield:** 6 servings

Ingredients
- 1 pound dried thin rice noodles
- 4 cups very hot water
- 1 tablespoon vegetable oil
- ¾ cup firm tofu, cubed
- ¼ cup fresh basil leaves
- 2 tablespoons vegetable oil
- ¾ cup chicken, cut into cubes
- ½ cup small black tiger shrimp, peeled and deveined

- 1 ½ teaspoons paprika
- 2 large eggs eggs, beaten
- 7 tablespoons vegetable oil
- 3 cloves garlic, minced
- ½ cup white vinegar
- ½ cup fish sauce
- 1 tablespoon brown sugar
- 2 teaspoons ketchup
- 2 teaspoons tamarind paste
- 1 teaspoon hot chili sauce (such as Sriracha®)
- 2 stalk (blank)s lemon grass stalks, minced
- ½ cup water, if needed
- 3 tablespoons chopped roasted peanuts
- 1 cup bean sprouts
- 1 lime, cut in wedges
- 4 eaches green onions, thinly sliced

Directions

- **Step 1**

  Soak rice noodles in a bowl with 4 cups hot water, or as needed to cover, until noodles are slightly softened, about 15 minutes; drain.

- **Step 2**

  Heat 1 tablespoon vegetable oil in a wok over medium heat.

- **Step 3**

  Cook and stir tofu and basil leaves in hot oil until basil is crisp and tofu is golden, about 10 minutes. Remove tofu-basil mixture and set aside.

- **Step 4**

  Heat 2 tablespoons vegetable oil in the same skillet; cook and stir chicken, shrimp and paprika until chicken is no longer pink in the center and shrimp are bright pink on the outside and no longer transparent in the center, 5 to 8 minutes.

- **Step 5**

  Pour eggs into chicken and shrimp; stir until eggs are lightly cooked, 2 to 3 minutes. Remove and set aside.

- **Step 6**

  Heat 7 tablespoons vegetable oil in a clean wok over medium heat. Cook and stir garlic in hot oil until fragrant, a few seconds.

- **Step 7**

  Stir white vinegar, fish sauce, brown sugar, ketchup, tamarind paste, and hot chili sauce into garlic until the brown sugar has dissolved; simmer for 1 minute.

- **Step 8**

    Stir lemon grass and drained rice noodles into wok until sauce is almost absorbed, 2 to 3 minutes. Pour 1/2 cup water into the skillet if noodles are still too firm.

- **Step 9**

    Stir tofu with basil, peanuts, chicken and shrimp mixture, and bean sprouts into noodles; cook and stir until fully heated and combined with sauce, 1 to 2 minutes.

- **Step 10**

    Garnish with lime wedges and green onions.

Nutrition Facts

Per Serving:

560.1 calories; protein 16.8g 34% DV; carbohydrates 58.3g 19% DV; fat 29.3g 45% DV; cholesterol 93.8mg 31% DV; sodium 1652.8mg 66% DV.

Spence's Secret Thai Red Shrimp Curry

Prep: 20 mins **Cook:** 20 mins **Total:** 40 mins **Servings:** 4 **Yield:** 4 servings

Ingredients

- 2 tablespoons sesame oil
- 1 ½ tablespoons red curry paste, or more to taste
- 1 red onion, cut into 1/2-inch dice
- 2 large bell peppers, cut into 3/4-inch pieces
- 2 (14 ounce) cans coconut milk
- ½ cup chicken broth
- 3 ½ tablespoons maple syrup
- 3 tablespoons fish sauce
- 3 stalks lemon grass, bruised and chopped
- 4 leaf (blank)s kaffir lime leaves, torn into quarters
- 1 pound medium shrimp, peeled and deveined
- ¼ cup packed chopped fresh basil
- 2 tablespoons chopped fresh cilantro

Directions

- **Step 1**

    Heat oil in a wok over medium-high heat; stir in curry paste and cook until fragrant, about 1 minute. Stir onion into curry paste; cook until just tender, about 3 minutes. Stir in peppers; cook and stir for 3 more minutes.

- **Step 2**

Stir coconut milk, chicken broth, maple syrup, fish sauce, lemon grass, and lime leaves into vegetable mixture. Bring curry to a boil; reduce heat to low and simmer until vegetables are tender, about 8 minutes. Stir in shrimp; cook until shrimp is pink at the center, about 5 minutes.

- **Step 3**

    Remove wok from heat; stir basil and cilantro into curry. Serve hot.

Cook's Notes:

Optional additional veggies such as chopped broccoli or zucchini can be added or substituted.

Fresh lime leaves can be frozen in an airtight freezer bag for up to 6 months.

If lemon grass is not very tender it can be tied into a bundle using cheesecloth before being added to the sauce (it saves picking out woody lemon grass pieces).

Nutrition Facts

Per Serving:

632.8 calories; protein 24.5g 49% DV; carbohydrates 29g 9% DV; fat 49.9g 77% DV; cholesterol 173.2mg 58% DV; sodium 1279.3mg 51% DV.

Wat Wah Tat

Prep: 20 mins **Cook:** 15 mins **Total:** 35 mins **Servings:** 6 **Yield:** 6 servings

Ingredients

- 3 tablespoons vegetable oil
- 2 medium (4-1/8" long)s green onions, thinly sliced
- 2 cloves garlic, minced
- 1 garlic scape, chopped
- ½ pound extra-firm tofu, cubed
- ¼ cup fermented black beans
- ¼ cup mushroom oyster sauce
- 1 cup water
- 1 tablespoon rice vinegar
- 1 tablespoon tamari sauce
- ¼ teaspoon ground ginger
- 2 cups dried shiitake mushrooms
- ½ pound fresh spinach, chopped

Directions

- **Step 1**

    Heat the vegetable oil in a wok or large skillet over medium-high heat. Stir in the green onions, garlic, and garlic scape; cook and stir until the vegetables have softened, about 30 seconds. Stir in the toru, black beans, mushroom oyster sauce, and half of the water. Cover, and bring to a boil. Cook 3 minutes.

- **Step 2**

Stir in the remaining water, rice vinegar, tamari sauce, and ginger. Add the mushrooms (the mushrooms will reconstitute in the sauce while cooking) and top with spinach. Recover, and turn the heat to low. Simmer until the spinach has wilted and the mushrooms are tender, about 10 minutes.

Nutrition Facts

Per Serving:

270.3 calories; protein 11.5g 23% DV; carbohydrates 41.5g 13% DV; fat 10.2g 16% DV; cholesterolmg; sodium 281.7mg 11% DV.

Fettuccine Bombay

Prep: 20 mins **Cook:** 40 mins **Total:** 1 hr **Servings:** 4 **Yield:** 4 servings

Ingredients

- 1 (16 ounce) package fettuccine
- 3 tablespoons olive oil
- 1 teaspoon cumin seeds
- 1 large onion, chopped
- 4 cloves garlic, crushed
- 2 eaches skinless, boneless chicken breasts, cut into cubes
- 2 tablespoons curry powder, divided
- 1 (14 ounce) can diced tomatoes
- 2 tablespoons tomato paste

Directions

- **Step 1**

Bring a large pot of lightly-salted water to a rolling boil over high heat; add the fettuccine and return to a boil. Cook uncovered until the pasta has cooked through, but is still firm to the bite, about 8 minutes; drain.

- **Step 2**

Heat the olive oil in a large skillet or wok over medium-high heat. Fry the cumin seeds in the hot oil until they begin to pop, 2 to 3 minutes. Cook and stir the onion and garlic in the oil until lightly browned, about 5 minutes. Add the chicken and continue cooking until the chicken is cooked through, 4 to 5 minutes. Season with 1 tablespoon curry powder; cook and stir another 3 to 4 minutes. Pour the diced tomatoes over the mixture and reduce heat to low. Stir in the tomato paste and remaining 1 tablespoon curry powder. Simmer 15 minutes.

- **Step 3**

Stir the cooked pasta into the sauce to coat. Simmer 2 to 5 minutes, until pasta is reheated.

Nutrition Facts

Per Serving:

667.7 calories; protein 31.4g 63% DV; carbohydrates 99.1g 32% DV; fat 15.2g 23% DV; cholesterol 34.6mg 12% DV; sodium 257.5mg 10% DV.

Vegetarian Thai Fried Rice (Khao Pad Je)

Prep: 15 mins **Cook:** 10 mins **Total:** 25 mins **Servings:** 4 **Yield:** 4 servings

Ingredients

- 2 tablespoons vegetable oil, or more as needed
- ½ onion, chopped
- 9 ounces firm tofu, crumbled
- 1 cup peas
- 1 cup chopped tomatoes
- 4 cups cooked jasmine rice
- 2 tablespoons light soy sauce
- 2 teaspoons dark sweet soy sauce
- 3 eaches eggs
- 1 teaspoon soy-based liquid seasoning (such as Maggi®)
- 1 cup pineapple chunks, drained
- ¼ teaspoon ground white pepper

Directions

- **Step 1**

  Heat 1 tablespoon vegetable oil in a wok or large skillet over high heat. Cook onion and tofu until lightly browned, 3 to 5 minutes. Add peas and tomatoes and cook for 1 minute. Stir in rice and a little more oil if necessary to keep the rice from sticking. Stir-fry for 1 minute. Season with light soy sauce and sweet soy sauce; stir well.

- **Step 2**

  Move rice to one side of the wok or skillet and add remaining 1 tablespoon of vegetable oil to the empty side. Crack eggs into the skillet and season with soy seasoning. Let eggs cook for about 3 minutes; flip and scramble. Stir into rice mixture.

- **Step 3**

  Stir in pineapple until warmed through. Season with white pepper. Taste and adjust seasoning if needed.

Cook's Note:

You can also use brown rice instead of white.

Nutrition Facts

Per Serving:

448.3 calories; protein 16.8g 34% DV; carbohydrates 65.1g 21% DV; fat 13.9g 21% DV; cholesterol 122.8mg 41% DV; sodium 589.9mg 24% DV.

Japanese Spicy Spare Ribs

Prep: 30 mins **Cook:** 16 mins **Total:** 46 mins **Servings:** 4 **Yield:** 4 servings

Ingredients

- 1 pinch salt and ground black pepper to taste
- 1 pound pork spare ribs
- 1 tablespoon oil
- ¼ stalk celery, grated
- 1 (1/4 inch thick) slice fresh ginger, grated
- ½ clove garlic, grated
- 2 tablespoons soy sauce
- 1 fresh chile pepper, finely chopped
- 1 tablespoon sake
- 1 tablespoon tomato puree
- 1 tablespoon white sugar
- 1 teaspoon balsamic vinegar
- 1 pinch salt to taste

Directions

- **Step 1**

  Set oven rack about 6 inches from the heat source and preheat the oven's broiler. Line a baking sheet with aluminum foil; set a baking rack on top.

- **Step 2**

  Rub salt and pepper over the pork ribs; place on the prepared baking sheet.

- **Step 3**

  Cook in the preheated oven, flipping once, until meat pulls away easily from the bone, 7 to 10 minutes per side. An instant-read thermometer inserted into the center should read 145 degrees F (63 degrees C).

- **Step 4**

  Heat oil in a large skillet or wok over medium heat. Add celery, ginger, and garlic; cook and stir until fragrant, 2 to 3 minutes. Reduce heat to low. Mix in soy sauce, chile pepper, sake, tomato puree, sugar, balsamic vinegar, and salt; stir until sauce is combined. Remove from heat.

- **Step 5**

  Toss pork ribs in sauce until coated.

Cook's Notes:

Black vinegar can be substituted for the balsamic vinegar if desired.

You can bake the ribs on a baking sheet lined with aluminum foil, for 20 minutes, flipping halfway, at 350 degrees F (175 degrees C). An instant-read thermometer inserted into the center should read 145 degrees F (63 degrees C).

Nutrition Facts
Per Serving:
256.2 calories; protein 15.3g 31% DV; carbohydrates 5.8g 2% DV; fat 18.5g 28% DV; cholesterol 59.9mg 20% DV; sodium 593.5mg 24% DV.

Easy-Peezy Caramel Granola

Prep: 10 mins **Cook:** 5 mins **Additional:** 15 mins **Total:** 30 mins **Servings:** 8 **Yield:** 4 cups

Ingredients
- 2 cups quick cooking oats
- 1 cup brown sugar
- 2 tablespoons ground cinnamon
- ½ cup butter, melted
- 5 tablespoons caramel sauce
- 2 tablespoons white sugar

Directions
- **Step 1**

  Stir together the oats, brown sugar, and cinnamon in a wok or large skillet over high heat, cook 5 to 10 minutes; remove from heat and add the butter and caramel sauce; stir until evenly coated. Spread the mixture onto a flat platter or baking sheet in a thin layer. Sprinkle the white sugar over the granola. Allow to cool completely before serving.

Nutrition Facts
Per Serving:
331.6 calories; protein 3.1g 6% DV; carbohydrates 53.7g 17% DV; fat 12.9g 20% DV; cholesterol 30.6mg 10% DV; sodium 135.5mg 5% DV.

Nicola's Pad Thai

Prep: 15 mins **Cook:** 15 mins **Additional:** 8 hrs **Total:** 8 hrs 30 mins **Servings:** 4 **Yield:** 4 servings

Ingredients
- 2 cups pad Thai rice noodles, soaked in water overnight and drained
- ½ cup vegetable broth
- 2 tablespoons vegetable oil
- 1 tablespoon brown sugar
- 1 tablespoon soy sauce
- 1 tablespoon rice wine vinegar

- 1 ½ teaspoons peanut butter
- 1 teaspoon chopped fresh cilantro
- 1 teaspoon onion powder
- 1 teaspoon tamarind paste
- 1 teaspoon hot chile paste
- ¾ teaspoon garlic powder
- ½ teaspoon sesame oil
- ½ teaspoon crushed red pepper flakes
- ¼ teaspoon ground coriander
- ¼ teaspoon ground ginger
- 1 pinch salt and ground black pepper to taste
- 3 tablespoons vegetable oil
- ⅓ cup chopped broccoli
- ⅓ cup chopped carrots
- ⅓ cup snow peas, trimmed
- ⅓ cup sliced water chestnuts, drained
- ⅓ cup baby corn, drained
- ⅓ cup sliced fresh mushrooms
- ⅓ cup sliced zucchini
- 1 tablespoon vegetable oil
- 1 tablespoon chopped peanuts for topping
- 1 tablespoon chopped cilantro
- 1 pinch paprika for garnish

Directions

- **Step 1**
  Soak uncooked noodles in 8 cups of water until soft, 8 hours or overnight.
- **Step 2**
  Drain rice noodles and set aside.
- **Step 3**
  Whisk together vegetable broth, 2 tablespoons vegetable oil, brown sugar, soy sauce, rice wine vinegar, peanut butter, 1 teaspoon fresh cilantro, onion powder, tamarind paste, hot chile paste, garlic powder, sesame oil, red pepper flakes, ground coriander, ground ginger, salt, and ground black pepper in a saucepan.
- **Step 4**
  Heat sauce over medium heat until it bubbles; reduce heat to low, and simmer sauce while you prepare the remaining ingredients.
- **Step 5**

Heat 3 tablespoons of vegetable oil in a large wok over medium heat.
- **Step 6**
Cook and stir broccoli, carrots, snow peas, water chestnuts, baby corn, mushrooms, and zucchini in the wok until tender, 8 to 10 minutes.
- **Step 7**
Add the drained noodles and 1 tablespoon vegetable oil to vegetables. Cook and stir until noodles are heated through, 2 to 3 minutes.
- **Step 8**
Remove the wok from heat and pour the sauce over vegetables and rice noodles.
- **Step 9**
Toss to fully coat the vegetables and rice noodles with sauce.
- **Step 10**
Garnish with peanuts, 2 tablespoons chopped cilantro, and paprika.

Cook's Note:
Everyone has a different idea of what pad Thai should taste like, this is as close (vegan) as I have come to my favorite restaurant's take on this wonderful dish. I hope you enjoy.

Nutrition Facts
Per Serving:
519.6 calories; protein 5.1g 10% DV; carbohydrates 70.9g 23% DV; fat 24.2g 37% DV; cholesterolmg; sodium 467.3mg 19% DV.

Almond Vegetable Stir-Fry

Total Time Prep/Total Time: 20 min. Makes 5 servings

Ingredients
- 1 teaspoon cornstarch
- 1 teaspoon sugar
- 3 tablespoons cold water
- 2 tablespoons reduced-sodium soy sauce
- 1 teaspoon sesame oil
- 4 cups fresh broccoli florets
- 2 tablespoons canola oil
- 1 large sweet red pepper, cut into 1-inch chunks
- 1 small onion, cut into thin wedges
- 2 garlic cloves, minced

- 1 tablespoon minced fresh gingerroot
- 1/4 cup slivered almonds, toasted

Directions
- In a small bowl, combine cornstarch and sugar. Stir in water, soy sauce and sesame oil until smooth; set aside.
- In a large nonstick wok or skillet, stir-fry broccoli in hot oil 3 minutes. Add pepper, onion, garlic and ginger; stir-fry 2 minutes. Reduce heat. Stir soy sauce mixture; stir into vegetables with nuts. Cook and stir 2 minutes or until thickened.

Nutrition Facts
3/4 cup: 143 calories, 10g fat (1g saturated fat), 0 cholesterol, 260mg sodium, 11g carbohydrate (0 sugars, 3g fiber), 4g protein.

Asian Pork Linguine

Total Time Prep/Total Time: 30 min. Makes 5 servings

Ingredients
- 6 ounces uncooked linguine
- 2 teaspoons cornstarch
- 1/2 cup water
- 1/4 cup reduced-fat creamy peanut butter
- 2 tablespoons reduced-sodium soy sauce
- 1 tablespoon honey
- 1/2 teaspoon garlic powder
- 1/8 teaspoon ground ginger
- 1 pound boneless pork loin chops, cubed
- 3 teaspoons sesame oil, divided
- 2 medium carrots, sliced
- 1 medium onion, halved and sliced

Directions
- Cook linguine according to package directions. For sauce, in a small bowl, combine cornstarch and water until smooth. Whisk in the peanut butter, soy sauce, honey, garlic powder and ginger until blended; set aside.
- In a large nonstick skillet or wok, stir-fry pork in 2 teaspoons oil until no longer pink. Remove and keep warm. Stir-fry carrots and onion in remaining oil until crisp-tender. Stir the sauce and add to the pan. Bring to a boil; cook and stir until thickened, about 2 minutes.
- Return pork to the pan. Drain linguine; add to the pan and stir to coat.

Nutrition Facts

1 cup: 376 calories, 13g fat (3g saturated fat), 44mg cholesterol, 358mg sodium, 39g carbohydrate (9g sugars, 3g fiber), 27g protein. **Diabetic Exchanges:** 3 lean meat, 2-1/2 starch, 2 fat.

Vegetable Pad Thai

Total Time Prep: 25 min. Cook: 15 min. Makes 6 servings

Ingredients
- 1 package (12 ounces) whole wheat fettuccine
- 1/4 cup rice vinegar
- 3 tablespoons reduced-sodium soy sauce
- 2 tablespoons brown sugar
- 2 tablespoons fish sauce or additional reduced-sodium soy sauce
- 1 tablespoon lime juice
- Dash Louisiana-style hot sauce
- 1 package (12 ounces) extra-firm tofu, drained and cut into 1/2-inch cubes
- 3 teaspoons canola oil, divided
- 2 medium carrots, grated
- 2 cups fresh snow peas, halved
- 3 garlic cloves, minced
- 2 large eggs, lightly beaten
- 2 cups bean sprouts
- 3 green onions, chopped
- 1/2 cup minced fresh cilantro
- 1/4 cup unsalted peanuts, chopped

Directions
- Cook fettuccine according to package directions. Meanwhile, in a small bowl, combine the vinegar, soy sauce, brown sugar, fish sauce, lime juice and hot sauce until smooth; set aside.
- In a large skillet or wok, stir-fry tofu in 2 teaspoons oil until golden brown. Remove and keep warm. Stir-fry carrots and snow peas in remaining oil for 1-2 minutes. Add garlic; cook 1 minute longer or until vegetables are crisp-tender. Add eggs; cook and stir until set.
- Drain pasta; add to vegetable mixture. Stir vinegar mixture and add to the skillet. Bring to a boil. Add tofu, bean sprouts and onions; heat through. Sprinkle with cilantro and peanuts.

Nutrition Facts
1-1/3 cups: 383 calories, 11g fat (2g saturated fat), 71mg cholesterol, 806mg sodium, 61g carbohydrate (11g sugars, 10g fiber), 18g protein.

Peanut Chicken Stir-Fry

Total Time Prep/Total Time: 30 min. Makes 4 servings

Ingredients
- 1/2 cup plus 1 tablespoon water, divided
- 1/4 cup peanut butter
- 3 tablespoons soy sauce
- 1 tablespoon brown sugar
- 2 to 3 garlic cloves, minced
- 2 tablespoons canola oil
- 1 pound boneless skinless chicken breasts, cubed
- 3 cups fresh broccoli florets
- 1 tablespoon cornstarch
- Hot cooked rice or noodles

Directions
- In a small bowl, combine 1/2 cup water, peanut butter, soy sauce and brown sugar until smooth; set aside. In a skillet or wok, stir-fry garlic in oil for 30 seconds. Add the chicken; stir-fry for 5 minutes or until no longer pink. Add the broccoli; stir-fry for 5 minutes.
- Stir in the peanut butter mixture; cook and stir for 2-3 minutes or until sauce is smooth and broccoli is crisp-tender. Combine cornstarch and remaining water until smooth; gradually add to skillet. Bring to a boil; cook and stir for 2 minutes or until thickened. Serve with rice or noodles.

Nutrition Facts
1 cup: 322 calories, 18g fat (3g saturated fat), 63mg cholesterol, 835mg sodium, 12g carbohydrate (6g sugars, 3g fiber), 30g protein.

Thai Beef Stir-Fry

Total Time Prep: 20 min. Cook: 20 min. Makes 6 servings

Ingredients
- 1/2 cup packed brown sugar
- 2 tablespoons cornstarch
- 2 cups beef broth
- 1/3 cup reduced-sodium soy sauce
- 1 teaspoon onion powder
- 1 teaspoon garlic powder
- 1 teaspoon ground ginger
- 1/4 teaspoon hot pepper sauce
- 2 pounds boneless beef sirloin steak, cut into thin strips

- 6 tablespoons olive oil, divided
- 4 cups fresh broccoli florets
- 2 cups fresh cauliflowerets
- 1-1/2 cups julienned carrots
- 2 cups sliced fresh mushrooms
- 1/4 cup peanut butter
- Hot cooked spaghetti
- 1/2 cup chopped peanuts

Directions

- In a small bowl, combine the first 8 ingredients until smooth; set aside. In a large cast-iron skillet or wok, stir-fry beef in 3 tablespoons oil until meat is no longer pink. Remove and keep warm.
- In the same skillet, stir-fry broccoli, cauliflower and carrots in remaining oil for 5 minutes. Add mushrooms; stir-fry until the vegetables are crisp-tender, 3-5 minutes.
- Stir broth mixture and add to the pan. Bring to a boil; cook and stir until thickened, about 2 minutes. Reduce heat; add beef and peanut butter. Cook and stir over medium heat until peanut butter is blended. Serve with spaghetti. Sprinkle with peanuts.
  Freeze option: Do not cook spaghetti. Freeze cooled beef mixture in freezer containers. To use, partially thaw in refrigerator overnight. Cook spaghetti according to package directions. Place beef mixture in a large skillet and heat through, stirring occasionally; add a little broth if necessary. Serve with spaghetti and sprinkle with peanuts.

Nutrition Facts

1 cup: 586 calories, 32g fat (6g saturated fat), 61mg cholesterol, 974mg sodium, 35g carbohydrate (22g sugars, 5g fiber), 42g protein.

Sirloin Stir-Fry with Ramen Noodles

Total Time Prep/Total Time: 30 min. Makes 4 servings

Ingredients

- 2 packages (3 ounces each) beef ramen noodles
- 2 tablespoons cornstarch
- 2 cups beef broth, divided
- 1 pound beef top sirloin steak, cut into thin strips
- 2 tablespoons canola oil
- 2 tablespoons reduced-sodium soy sauce
- 2 cans (14 ounces each) whole baby corn, rinsed and drained
- 2 cups fresh broccoli florets
- 1 cup diced sweet red pepper
- 1 cup shredded carrots

- 4 green onions, cut into 1-inch pieces
- 1/2 cup unsalted peanuts

Directions

- Set aside seasoning packets from noodles. Cook noodles according to package directions.
- Meanwhile, in a small bowl, combine cornstarch and 1/4 cup broth until smooth; set aside. In a large skillet or wok, stir-fry beef in oil until no longer pink. Add soy sauce; cook until liquid has evaporated, 3-4 minutes. Remove beef and keep warm.
- Add the corn, broccoli, red pepper, carrots, onions and remaining broth to the pan. Sprinkle with contents of seasoning packets. Stir-fry until vegetables are crisp-tender, 5-7 minutes.
- Stir the cornstarch mixture and add to skillet. Bring to a boil; cook and stir until thickened, about 2 minutes. Drain noodles. Add beef and noodles to pan; heat through. Garnish with peanuts.

Nutrition Facts

1-1/2 cups: 593 calories, 28g fat (8g saturated fat), 46mg cholesterol, 2022mg sodium, 49g carbohydrate (8g sugars, 8g fiber), 38g protein.

Sweet-and-Sour Beef

Total Time Prep/Total Time: 30 min. Makes 4 servings

Ingredients

- 1 tablespoon cornstarch
- 2 tablespoons cold water
- 1 pound beef top sirloin steak, cut into 1/2-inch cubes
- 1 teaspoon salt
- 1/2 teaspoon pepper
- 3 teaspoons canola oil, divided
- 1 large green pepper, cut into 1/2-inch pieces
- 1 large sweet red pepper, cut into 1/2-inch pieces
- 2 medium tart apples, chopped
- 1/2 cup plus 2 tablespoons thinly sliced green onions, divided
- 2/3 cup packed brown sugar
- 1/2 cup cider vinegar
- Hot cooked rice, optional

Directions

- In a small bowl, mix cornstarch and water until smooth. Sprinkle beef with salt and pepper. In a large nonstick skillet or wok coated with cooking spray, heat 2 teaspoons oil over medium-high heat. Add beef; stir-fry 2-3 minutes or until no longer pink. Remove from pan.
- In same skillet, stir-fry peppers and apples in remaining oil for 2 minutes. Add 1/2 cup green onions; stir-fry 1-3 minutes longer or until peppers are crisp-tender. Remove from pan.

- Add brown sugar and vinegar to skillet; bring to a boil, stirring to dissolve sugar. Stir cornstarch mixture and add to pan. Return to a boil; cook and stir 1-2 minutes or until thickened. Return beef and pepper mixture to pan; heat through. If desired, serve with rice. Sprinkle with remaining green onion.

Nutrition Facts

1-1/2 cups (calculated without rice): 389 calories, 8g fat (2g saturated fat), 46mg cholesterol, 663mg sodium, 53g carbohydrate (46g sugars, 4g fiber), 25g protein.

Simple Shrimp Pad Thai

Total Time Prep/Total Time: 30 min. Makes 4 servings

Ingredients

- 8 ounces uncooked thick rice noodles
- 1 pound uncooked medium shrimp, peeled and deveined
- 3 garlic cloves, minced
- 2 tablespoons canola oil
- 2 large eggs, beaten
- 1 cup marinara sauce
- 1/4 cup reduced-sodium soy sauce
- 2 tablespoons brown sugar
- 1/4 cup chopped dry roasted peanuts

Fresh cilantro leaves

- 1 medium lime, cut into wedges
- Sriracha chili sauce or hot pepper sauce, optional

Directions

- Cook noodles according to package directions.
- Meanwhile, stir-fry shrimp and garlic in oil in a large nonstick skillet or wok until shrimp turn pink; remove and keep warm. Add eggs to skillet; cook and stir until set.
- Add the marinara, soy sauce and brown sugar; heat through. Return shrimp to the pan. Drain noodles; toss with shrimp mixture.
- Sprinkle with peanuts and cilantro. Serve with lime and, if desired, Sriracha.

Nutrition Facts

1-1/4 cups (caluculated without sriracha): 530 calories, 17g fat (2g saturated fat), 232mg cholesterol, 1212mg sodium, 64g carbohydrate (11g sugars, 3g fiber), 29g protein.

Turkey Asparagus Stir-Fry

Total Time Prep/Total Time: 20 min. Makes 5 servings

Ingredients
- 1 tablespoon olive oil
- 1 pound boneless skinless turkey breast halves, cut into strips
- 1 pound fresh asparagus, cut into 1-inch pieces
- 4 ounces fresh mushrooms, sliced
- 2 medium carrots, quartered lengthwise and cut into 1-inch pieces
- 4 green onions, cut into 1-inch pieces
- 2 garlic cloves, minced
- 1/2 teaspoon ground ginger
- 2/3 cup cold water
- 2 tablespoons reduced-sodium soy sauce
- 4 teaspoons cornstarch
- 1 can (8 ounces) sliced water chestnuts, drained
- 3-1/2 cups hot cooked white or brown rice
- 1 medium tomato, cut into wedges

Directions
- In a large skillet or wok, heat oil over medium-high heat. Add turkey; stir-fry until no longer pink, about 5 minutes. Remove and keep warm.
- Add next six ingredients to pan; stir-fry until vegetables are crisp-tender, about 5 minutes. Combine water, soy sauce and cornstarch; add to skillet with water chestnuts. Bring to a boil; cook and stir 1-2 minutes or until sauce is thickened. Return turkey to skillet and heat through. Serve with rice and tomato wedges.

Nutrition Facts
1 cup with 3/4 cup rice: 343 calories, 5g fat (1g saturated fat), 52mg cholesterol, 363mg sodium, 47g carbohydrate (4g sugars, 4g fiber), 28g protein. **Diabetic Exchanges:** 3 starch, 3 lean meat, 1 vegetable, 1/2 fat.

Colorful Shrimp Pad Thai

Total Time Prep: 30 min. Cook: 15 min. Makes 6 servings

Ingredients
- 6 ounces uncooked thick rice noodles
- 1/4 cup rice vinegar
- 3 tablespoons reduced-sodium soy sauce
- 2 tablespoons sugar
- 2 tablespoons fish sauce or additional reduced-sodium soy sauce

- 1 tablespoon lime juice
- 2 teaspoons Thai chili sauce
- 1 teaspoon sesame oil
- 1/4 teaspoon crushed red pepper flakes

STIR-FRY:
- 1-1/2 pounds uncooked medium shrimp, peeled and deveined
- 3 teaspoons sesame oil, divided
- 2 cups fresh snow peas
- 2 medium carrots, grated
- 2 garlic cloves, minced
- 2 large eggs, lightly beaten
- 2 cups bean sprouts
- 2 green onions, chopped
- 1/4 cup minced fresh cilantro
- 1/4 cup unsalted dry roasted peanuts, chopped

Directions

Cook noodles according to package directions. Meanwhile, in a small bowl, combine the vinegar, soy sauce, sugar, fish sauce, lime juice, chili sauce, oil and pepper flakes until blended; set aside.

In a large nonstick skillet or wok, stir-fry shrimp in 2 teaspoons oil until shrimp turn pink; remove and keep warm. Stir-fry snow peas and carrots in remaining oil for 1-2 minutes. Add garlic, cook 1 minute longer or until vegetables are crisp-tender. Add eggs; cook and stir until set.

Drain noodles; add to vegetable mixture. Stir vinegar mixture and add to the skillet. Bring to a boil. Add shrimp, bean sprouts and green onions; heat through. Sprinkle with cilantro and peanuts.

Nutrition Facts

1 cup: 352 calories, 10g fat (2g saturated fat), 208mg cholesterol, 955mg sodium, 38g carbohydrate (10g sugars, 4g fiber), 28g protein.

Saucy Thai Beef Noodles

Total Time Prep/Total Time: 30 min. Makes 6 servings

Ingredients
- 1/2 cup 2% milk
- 1/2 cup creamy peanut butter
- 1/4 cup soy sauce
- 2 tablespoons brown sugar
- 2 tablespoons sherry
- 2 garlic cloves, minced

- 1/4 teaspoon crushed red pepper flakes
- 3 drops hot pepper sauce
- 12 ounces uncooked spaghetti
- 1 pound beef top sirloin steak, thinly sliced
- 1-1/2 teaspoons canola oil, divided
- 1/2 cup thinly sliced fresh carrot
- 1/2 cup julienned sweet red pepper
- 1 cup fresh snow peas
- 2 green onions, sliced
- 1/4 cup chopped salted peanuts
- 2 tablespoons minced fresh cilantro

Directions
- In a small saucepan, bring the first eight ingredients just to a boil, stirring constantly. Remove from the heat; set aside.
- Cook spaghetti according to package directions.
- In a large skillet or wok, stir-fry beef in 1/2 teaspoon oil until no longer pink. Remove and keep warm.
- Stir-fry carrot and red pepper in remaining oil for 3-4 minutes. Add snow peas and onions; stir-fry 2-3 minutes longer or until vegetables are crisp-tender. Return beef to skillet.
- Drain noodles; add to the pan. Add peanut sauce and toss to coat. Sprinkle with peanuts and cilantro.

Nutrition Facts

1-1/3 cups: 536 calories, 19g fat (4g saturated fat), 31mg cholesterol, 795mg sodium, 58g carbohydrate (11g sugars, 5g fiber), 34g protein.

Goong Tod Kratiem Prik Thai (Prawns Fried with Garlic and White Pepper)

Prep: 5 mins **Cook:** 4 mins **Total:** 9 mins **Servings:** 4 **Yield:** 1 pound

Ingredients
- 8 cloves garlic, chopped, or more to taste
- 2 tablespoons tapioca flour
- 2 tablespoons fish sauce
- 2 tablespoons light soy sauce
- 1 tablespoon white sugar
- ½ teaspoon ground white pepper
- ¼ cup vegetable oil, divided, or as needed
- 1 pound whole unpeeled prawns, divided

Directions

- **Step 1**

    Combine garlic, tapioca flour, fish sauce, soy sauce, sugar, and white pepper in a bowl; add prawns and toss to coat.

- **Step 2**

    Heat 2 tablespoons oil in a heavy skillet over high heat. Add 1/2 of the prawns in single layer; fry until golden brown and crispy, 1 to 2 minutes per side. Repeat with remaining oil and remaining prawns.

Cook's Notes:

Use wok instead of skillet, if desired.

Prawns can be fried in 3 batches or more, if needed, depending on the size of your skillet or wok.

Nutrition Facts

Per Serving:

377.4 calories; protein 20.5g 41% DV; carbohydrates 19.5g 6% DV; fat 24.7g 38% DV; cholesterol 156.6mg 52% DV; sodium 1118.2mg 45% DV.

Tsao Mi Fun (Taiwanese Fried Rice Noodles)

Prep: 35 mins **Cook:** 15 mins **Additional:** 20 mins **Total:** 1 hr 10 mins **Servings:** 4 **Yield:** 4 servings

Ingredients

- ½ pound thinly sliced pork loin
- ¼ cup soy sauce
- ¼ cup rice wine
- 1 teaspoon white pepper
- 1 teaspoon Chinese five-spice powder
- 1 teaspoon cornstarch
- 4 eaches dried Chinese black mushrooms
- 1 (8 ounce) package dried rice vermicelli
- ¼ cup vegetable oil, divided
- 2 large eggs eggs, beaten
- ¼ clove garlic, minced
- 1 tablespoon dried small shrimp
- 3 carrot, (7-1/2")s carrots, cut into matchstick strips
- ½ onion, chopped
- 3 cups bean sprouts
- 4 leaves napa cabbage, thinly sliced
- 1 pinch salt to taste
- 3 sprigs fresh cilantro for garnish

Directions

- **Step 1**

  Place the pork into a mixing bowl and pour in the soy sauce and rice wine. Sprinkle with the white pepper, five-spice powder, and cornstarch. Mix well, then set aside to marinate. Soak the mushrooms in a bowl of cold water for 20 minutes, then pour off the water, cut off and discard the stems of the mushrooms. Slice the mushrooms thinly and reserve. Soak the rice vermicelli in a separate bowl of cold water for 10 minutes, then pour off the water and set the noodles aside.

- **Step 2**

  Heat 1 tablespoon of the vegetable oil in a wok or large skillet over medium heat. Pour in the eggs, and cook until firm, flipping once, to make a pancake. Remove the egg pancake, and allow to cool, then thinly slice and place into a large bowl. Heat 2 more tablespoons of the vegetable oil in the wok over high heat. Stir in the garlic and dried shrimp, and cook until the shrimp become aromatic, about 20 seconds. Next, add the pork along with the marinade, and cook until the pork is no longer pink, about 4 minutes. Stir in the carrots and onion, and cook until the carrots begin to soften, about 3 minutes. Finally, add the bean sprouts, napa cabbage, and sliced mushrooms; cook and stir until the vegetables are tender, about 3 minutes more. Scrape the pork mixture into the bowl along with the eggs, then wipe out the wok and return it to the stove over medium-high heat.

- **Step 3**

  Heat the remaining vegetable oil in the wok, then stir in the drained rice vermicelli noodles. Cook and stir for a few minutes until the noodles soften, then stir in the reserved pork mixture. Scrape the mixture in to a serving bowl and garnish with cilantro to serve.

Nutrition Facts

Per Serving:

523.2 calories; protein 19.2g 38% DV; carbohydrates 63g 20% DV; fat 20g 31% DV; cholesterol 122.1mg 41% DV; sodium 1106mg 44% DV.

Fiery Chicken Thigh Stir-Fry

Prep: 20 mins **Cook:** 20 mins **Total:** 40 mins **Servings:** 4 **Yield:** 4 servings

Ingredients

- ½ cup chopped onion
- ½ cup chopped red bell peppers
- ½ cup sliced fresh mushrooms
- ½ cup chopped green beans
- 2 ½ tablespoons sesame oil, divided
- 1 tablespoon rice vinegar
- 1 ½ teaspoons chili-garlic sauce
- 1 pound boneless skinless chicken thighs, cut into bite-size pieces
- 1 clove garlic, minced

- ½ teaspoon minced fresh ginger root
- 1 tablespoon everything bagel seasoning

Directions

- **Step 1**

Preheat the oven to 425 degrees F (220 degrees C). Line a rimmed baking sheet with aluminum foil.

- **Step 2**

Combine onion, bell pepper, mushrooms, green beans, and 1 tablespoon sesame oil; toss until well combined. Spread vegetables out on the prepared baking sheet.

- **Step 3**

Bake in the preheated oven for 15 minutes, turning vegetables after 8 minutes.

- **Step 4**

Heat remaining 1 1/2 tablespoons sesame oil in a wok over medium-high heat. Stir in rice vinegar and chili-garlic sauce. Add chicken, minced garlic, and ginger. Stir-fry for 5 minutes. Mix in roasted vegetables. Sprinkle with bagel seasoning before serving.

Nutrition Facts

Per Serving:

289.7 calories; protein 18.8g 38% DV; carbohydrates 4.9g 2% DV; fat 19.8g 31% DV; cholesterol 63.8mg 21% DV; sodium 382.2mg 15% DV.

Cashew Chicken with Water Chestnuts

Prep: 25 mins **Cook:** 15 mins **Total:** 40 mins **Servings:** 4 **Yield:** 4 servings

Ingredients

- 2 tablespoons cornstarch
- ⅔ cup chicken broth
- 3 tablespoons soy sauce
- ½ teaspoon ground ginger
- ½ teaspoon hot pepper sauce
- 2 tablespoons vegetable oil
- 1 pound skinless, boneless chicken breast meat - cut into strips
- 1 small onion, chopped
- 1 green bell pepper, chopped
- 1 (8 ounce) can sliced water chestnuts, drained
- ⅔ cup cashews

Directions

- **Step 1**

Dissolve the cornstarch in the chicken broth, and stir in the soy sauce, ginger, and hot sauce; set aside. Heat half of the oil in a wok or large skillet over high heat. Stir in the chicken; cook and stir until the chicken is no longer pink, about 5 minutes. Remove the chicken from the wok, and set aside.

- **Step 2**

Pour the remaining tablespoon of oil into the wok, and stir in the onion, green bell pepper, and water chestnuts. Cook and stir until the chestnuts are hot, and the onion has softened, about 5 minutes more. Stir up the sauce to redistribute the cornstarch, then pour into the wok, and bring to a boil. Add the reserved chicken, and stir until the sauce thickens, and the chicken is hot. Sprinkle with cashews to serve.

Nutrition Facts

Per Serving:

369.4 calories; protein 27.2g 55% DV; carbohydrates 22.1g 7% DV; fat 19.8g 31% DV; cholesterol 58.5mg 20% DV; sodium 892.4mg 36% DV.

Crispy Ginger Beef

Prep: 25 mins **Cook:** 20 mins **Total:** 45 mins **Servings:** 5 **Yield:** 5 cups

Ingredients

- ¾ cup cornstarch
- ½ cup water
- 2 large eggs eggs
- 1 pound flank steak, cut into thin strips
- ½ cup canola oil, or as needed
- 1 large carrot, cut into matchstick-size pieces
- 1 green bell pepper, cut into matchstick-size pieces
- 1 red bell pepper, cut into matchstick-size pieces
- 3 eaches green onions, chopped
- ¼ cup minced fresh ginger root
- 5 eaches garlic cloves, minced
- ½ cup white sugar
- ¼ cup rice vinegar
- 3 tablespoons soy sauce
- 1 tablespoon sesame oil
- 1 tablespoon red pepper flakes, or to taste

Directions

- **Step 1**

Place cornstarch in a large bowl; gradually whisk in water until smooth. Whisk eggs into cornstarch mixture; toss steak strips in mixture to coat.

- **Step 2**

  Pour canola oil into wok 1-inch deep; heat oil over high heat until hot but not smoking. Place 1/4 of the beef strips into hot oil; separate strips with a fork. Cook, stirring frequently, until coating is crisp and golden, about 3 minutes. Remove beef to drain on paper towels; repeat with remaining beef.

- **Step 3**

  Drain off all but 1 tablespoon oil; cook and stir carrot, green bell pepper, red bell pepper, green onions, ginger, and garlic over high heat until lightly browned but still crisp, about 3 minutes.

- **Step 4**

  Whisk sugar, rice vinegar, soy sauce, sesame oil, and red pepper together in a small bowl. Pour sauce mixture over vegetables in wok; bring mixture to a boil. Stir beef back into vegetable mixture; cook and stir just until heated through, about 3 minutes.

Cook's Note:

This is the original recipe but I like to add about 1/4 cup of teriyaki sauce as a variation. I also like to add sesame oil to the oil when I fry the beef.

Nutrition Facts

Per Serving:

364.3 calories; protein 15g 30% DV; carbohydrates 45.4g 15% DV; fat 13.8g 21% DV; cholesterol 102.9mg 34% DV; sodium 613.8mg 25% DV.

Super-Simple, Super-Spicy Mongolian Beef

Prep: 15 mins **Cook:** 6 mins **Additional:** 1 hr **Total:** 1 hr 21 mins **Servings:** 4 **Yield:** 4 servings

Ingredients

- ¼ cup soy sauce
- 1 tablespoon hoisin sauce
- 1 tablespoon sesame oil
- 2 teaspoons white sugar
- 1 tablespoon minced garlic
- 1 tablespoon red pepper flakes
- 1 pound beef flank steak, thinly sliced
- 1 tablespoon peanut oil
- 2 large green onions, thinly sliced

Directions

- **Step 1**

  Whisk together soy sauce, hoisin sauce, sesame oil, sugar, garlic, and red pepper flakes in a bowl. Toss beef with marinade, cover, and refrigerate 1 hour to overnight.

- **Step 2**

Heat peanut oil in a wok or large, nonstick skillet over high heat. Add the green onions, and cook for 5 to 10 seconds before stirring in the beef. Cook and stir until the beef is no longer pink and is beginning to brown, about 5 minutes.

Nutrition Facts

Per Serving:

199.5 calories; protein 15.4g 31% DV; carbohydrates 7.9g 3% DV; fat 11.9g 18% DV; cholesterol 25.4mg 9% DV; sodium 995.8mg 40% DV.

Caramelized Pork Belly (Thit Kho)

Prep: 20 mins **Cook:** 1 hr 13 mins **Additional:** 10 mins **Total:** 1 hr 43 mins **Servings:** 6 **Yield:** 6 servings

Ingredients

- 2 pounds pork belly, trimmed
- 2 tablespoons white sugar
- 5 eaches shallots, sliced
- 3 cloves garlic, chopped
- 3 tablespoons fish sauce
- 1 pinch ground black pepper to taste
- 13 fluid ounces coconut water
- 6 large eggs hard-boiled eggs, peeled

Directions

- **Step 1**

  Slice pork belly into 1-inch pieces layered with skin, fat, and meat.

- **Step 2**

  Heat sugar in a large wok or pot over medium heat until it melts and caramelizes into a light brown syrup, about 5 minutes. Add pork and increase heat to high. Cook and stir to render some of the pork fat, 3 to 5 minutes.

- **Step 3**

  Stir shallots and garlic into the wok. Add fish sauce and black pepper; stir to evenly coat pork. Pour in coconut water and bring to a boil. Add eggs, reduce heat to low, and simmer, covered, until pork is tender, about 1 hour.

- **Step 4**

  Remove wok from the heat and let stand, about 10 minutes. Skim the fat from the surface of the dish.

Cook's Note:

Check occasionally while the pork is simmering that the liquid doesn't evaporate too much. Add water a little at a time if sauce seems to be drying out.

Nutrition Facts

Per Serving:
410.3 calories; protein 26.7g 53% DV; carbohydrates 15.6g 5% DV; fat 26.3g 41% DV; cholesterol 266.8mg 89% DV; sodium 1831.6mg 73% DV.

Moo Goo Gai Pan

Prep: 25 mins **Cook:** 15 mins **Total:** 40 mins **Servings:** 3 **Yield:** 3 servings

Ingredients
- 1 tablespoon vegetable oil
- 1 cup sliced fresh mushrooms
- 2 cups chopped broccoli florets
- 1 (8 ounce) can sliced bamboo shoots, drained
- 1 (8 ounce) can sliced water chestnuts, drained
- 1 (15 ounce) can whole straw mushrooms, drained
- 1 tablespoon vegetable oil
- 2 cloves garlic, minced
- 1 pound skinless, boneless chicken breast, cut into strips
- 1 tablespoon cornstarch
- 1 tablespoon white sugar
- 1 tablespoon soy sauce
- 1 tablespoon oyster sauce
- 1 tablespoon rice wine
- ¼ cup chicken broth

Directions
- **Step 1**
  Heat 1 tablespoon of vegetable oil in a wok or large skillet over high heat until it begins to smoke. Stir in the fresh mushrooms, broccoli, bamboo shoots, water chestnuts, and straw mushrooms. Cook and stir until all the vegetables are hot, and the broccoli is tender, about 5 minutes. Remove from the wok, and set aside. Wipe out the wok.

- **Step 2**
  Heat the remaining tablespoon of vegetable in the wok until it begins to smoke. Stir in the garlic, and cook for a few seconds until it turns golden-brown. Add the chicken, and cook until the chicken has lightly browned on the edges, and is no longer pink in the center, about 5 minutes. Stir together the

cornstarch, sugar, soy sauce, oyster sauce, rice wine, and chicken broth in a small bowl. Pour over the chicken, and bring to a boil, stirring constantly. Boil for about 30 seconds until the sauce thickens and is no longer cloudy. Return the vegetables to the wok, and toss with the sauce.

Nutrition Facts

Per Serving:

409.2 calories; protein 41.7g 84% DV; carbohydrates 30.9g 10% DV; fat 14.3g 22% DV; cholesterol 86.3mg 29% DV; sodium 989.9mg 40% DV.

Orange Peel Beef

Prep: 25 mins **Cook:** 6 mins **Additional:** 1 hr **Total:** 1 hr 31 mins **Servings:** 6 **Yield:** 6 servings

Ingredients

- 1 ½ pounds beef top sirloin, thinly sliced
- 1 tablespoon low-sodium soy sauce
- 1 tablespoon cornstarch
- 1 teaspoon dark sesame oil
- ½ teaspoon baking soda
- 1 tablespoon low-sodium soy sauce
- 2 tablespoons frozen orange juice concentrate, thawed
- 1 tablespoon rice vinegar
- 1 teaspoon dark sesame oil
- 1 tablespoon brown sugar
- 1 teaspoon cornstarch
- 1 tablespoon peanut oil
- 3 cloves garlic, minced
- 1 tablespoon minced fresh ginger root
- 1 tablespoon finely shredded orange zest
- ¼ teaspoon red pepper flakes

Directions

- **Step 1**

Combine the beef, 1 tablespoon of soy sauce, 1 tablespoon cornstarch, 1 teaspoon sesame oil, and baking soda in a bowl and mix thoroughly. Cover and refrigerate 1 to 3 hours.

- **Step 2**

Heat peanut oil in a wok or large, nonstick skillet over high heat. Stir in garlic, ginger, orange zest, and red pepper flakes, and cook until the garlic begins to brown, 20 to 30 seconds. Add the beef; cook and stir until the beef begins to brown and crisp, about 5 minutes. Whisk together 1 tablespoon soy sauce, orange juice concentrate, rice vinegar, 1 teaspoon sesame oil, brown sugar, and 1 teaspoon cornstarch in a small bowl. Stir into the beef, and cook until the sauce has thickened and turned clear, about 30 seconds.

Nutrition Facts
Per Serving:

188.9 calories; protein 21.1g 42% DV; carbohydrates 7.5g 2% DV; fat 7.8g 12% DV; cholesterol 39mg 13% DV; sodium 326.3mg 13% DV.

Cashew Chicken Stir Fry

Prep: 25 mins **Cook:** 15 mins **Total:** 40 mins **Servings:** 4 **Yield:** 4 servings

Ingredients

- 4 eaches skinless, boneless chicken breast halves, cut into bite-size pieces
- 1 tablespoon Cajun seasoning blend (such as Tony Chachere's®), or to taste
- 1 ¼ cups chicken broth
- 1 tablespoon cornstarch
- 4 teaspoons soy sauce, divided
- 2 tablespoons olive oil, divided
- 2 cups shredded cabbage
- 25 eaches sugar snap peas, chopped
- 10 small spears fresh asparagus, trimmed and cut into bite-size pieces
- 3 stalks celery, chopped
- ½ red bell pepper, cut into thin strips
- 2 eaches green onions, chopped
- 1 (8 ounce) can sliced bamboo shoots, drained
- ½ cup cashews
- 1 pinch paprika, or to taste

Directions

- **Step 1**

Sprinkle chicken pieces with Cajun seasoning.

- **Step 2**

Whisk chicken broth, cornstarch, and 3 teaspoons soy sauce together in a bowl until completely blended.

- **Step 3**

Heat 1 tablespoon olive oil in a deep frying pan or wok over high heat. Cook and stir chicken in hot oil until cooked through, 6 to 10 minutes. Remove chicken from pan and drain any accumulated liquids.

- **Step 4**

Heat remaining 1 tablespoon olive oil in the frying pan or wok over high heat. Stir fry cabbage, snap peas, asparagus, celery, red bell pepper, green onions, and bamboo shoots for 1 minute. Stir in 1 teaspoon soy sauce. Continue cooking until vegetables are tender but still crisp, about 3 minutes.

- **Step 5**

Stir chicken into cabbage mixture. Pour chicken broth mixture over chicken mixture, reduce heat to medium, and simmer until sauce thickens, about 1 minute. Reduce heat to low; add cashews and cook until heated through, 1 minute. Sprinkle with paprika.

Nutrition Facts
Per Serving:
615.1 calories; protein 44.3g 89% DV; carbohydrates 61.8g 20% DV; fat 19g 29% DV; cholesterol 71.1mg 24% DV; sodium 1224.6mg 49% DV.

Pad Thai Quinoa Bowl

Prep: 30 mins **Cook:** 30 mins **Total:** 1 hr **Servings:** 8 **Yield:** 8 servings

Ingredients

- 4 cups low-sodium chicken broth
- 2 cups quinoa, rinsed and drained
- 1 tablespoon coconut oil, divided
- 1 large boneless, skinless chicken breast, cut into thin strips
- ¾ cup shredded cabbage
- ½ cup edamame
- ¼ cup diced broccoli stems
- 2 carrot, (7-1/2")s carrots, cut into matchsticks
- 2 eaches green onions, chopped
- 3 large eggs eggs
- 1 teaspoon sesame oil
- Thai peanut sauce:
- ¼ cup natural peanut butter
- ¼ cup reduced-sodium soy sauce
- 3 tablespoons rice vinegar
- 2 tablespoons chili garlic sauce
- 2 tablespoons chopped fresh ginger
- 3 cloves garlic, minced
- 1 teaspoon sesame oil
- ½ cup salted peanuts, chopped

- 3 tablespoons chopped fresh cilantro

Directions

- **Step 1**

  Bring chicken broth and quinoa to a boil in a saucepan. Reduce heat to medium-low, cover, and simmer until quinoa is tender, 15 to 20 minutes. Set aside.

- **Step 2**

  Heat 1 1/2 teaspoons coconut oil in a wok or large skillet over medium-high heat. Add chicken; stir until cooked through; about 5 minutes. Remove chicken from wok. Heat remaining 1 1/2 teaspoons coconut oil. Add cabbage, edamame, broccoli, carrot, and green onions and saute until vegetables soften slightly, 2 to 3 minutes.

- **Step 3**

  Whisk eggs with sesame oil in a small bowl. Push vegetables to the sides of the wok to make a well in the center; pour eggs in and stir to scramble, about 3 minutes.

- **Step 4**

  Combine peanut butter, soy sauce, rice vinegar, chili garlic sauce, ginger, garlic, and sesame oil together in a small bowl. Pour Thai peanut sauce over vegetable and egg mixture in the wok.

- **Step 5**

  Return chicken to the wok and add quinoa; mix well to combine. Stir in chopped peanuts and cilantro and serve.

Cook's Note:

You can tell when quinoa is cooked because it will increase in size and seem more transparent with a ribbon around the edges. Make sure all the liquid is cooked off.

Nutrition Facts

Per Serving:

369.6 calories; protein 20.9g 42% DV; carbohydrates 35.6g 12% DV; fat 16.8g 26% DV; cholesterol 87.9mg 29% DV; sodium 648.4mg 26% DV.

Healthier Pan-Fried Honey-Sesame Chicken

Prep: 15 mins **Cook:** 10 mins **Total:** 25 mins **Servings:** 4 **Yield:** 4 servings

Ingredients

Sauce:

- ½ cup water
- ⅓ cup low-sodium chicken broth
- ¼ cup ketchup
- ¼ cup low-sodium soy sauce
- ¼ cup honey
- 2 cloves garlic, crushed
- 1 tablespoon rice vinegar

- 2 teaspoons Sriracha sauce
- 2 teaspoons sesame oil
- 1 teaspoon grated fresh ginger root
- ¼ teaspoon crushed red pepper flakes, or to taste
- 2 tablespoons vegetable oil
- 4 eaches boneless chicken breast, cut into bite-size pieces
- 3 tablespoons water
- 2 tablespoons cornstarch

Directions
- **Step 1**

  Combine water, chicken broth, ketchup, soy sauce, honey, garlic, rice vinegar, Sriracha, sesame oil, ginger root, and red pepper flakes for sauce in a medium bowl.
- **Step 2**

  Heat vegetable oil in a wok or large skillet over medium-high heat. Add chicken, and stir-fry until chicken is opaque on all sides, 2 to 3 minutes. Transfer chicken to a plate.
- **Step 3**

  Reduce heat to medium and add the sauce to the wok. Whisk together water and cornstarch in a small bowl and add to the sauce, stirring constantly until the sauce starts to thicken, 3 to 5 minutes. Add chicken back to the wok, stir, and cook until reheated, about 2 minutes.

Nutrition Facts

Per Serving:

315.7 calories; protein 25.1g 50% DV; carbohydrates 27.3g 9% DV; fat 12.1g 19% DV; cholesterol 64.9mg 22% DV; sodium 880.1mg 35% DV.

Chinese Take-Out Shrimp with Garlic

Prep: 15 mins **Cook:** 10 mins **Total:** 25 mins **Servings:** 4 **Yield:** 4 servings

Ingredients
- 2 tablespoons canola oil
- 10 cloves garlic, chopped
- 1 teaspoon minced fresh ginger root
- 1 (8 ounce) can sliced water chestnuts, drained
- 1 cup snow peas
- 1 cup small white button mushrooms
- 1 teaspoon crushed red pepper flakes
- ½ teaspoon salt
- 1 teaspoon ground black pepper

- 1 pound peeled and deveined jumbo shrimp
- ½ cup chicken broth
- 1 tablespoon rice vinegar
- 2 tablespoons fish sauce
- 2 tablespoons dry sherry
- 1 tablespoon cornstarch
- 1 tablespoon water

Directions
- **Step 1**

    Heat oil in wok or large skillet until very hot. Cook and stir garlic and ginger in the hot oil until fragrant, about 30 seconds. Add the water chestnuts, snow peas, mushrooms, red pepper flakes, salt, pepper, and shrimp to the pan. Cook, stirring, until shrimp turns pink, 2 to 3 minutes.

- **Step 2**

    Combine the chicken broth, rice vinegar, fish sauce, and dry sherry in a small bowl. Pour into the shrimp mixture; cook and stir briefly to combine. Combine the cornstarch and water and stir into the wok. Stir until sauce has thickened, about 2 minutes.

Cook's Note:

If you really like it spicy, add up to 1 teaspoon additional crushed red pepper flakes.

Nutrition Facts

Per Serving:

225.5 calories; protein 21.4g 43% DV; carbohydrates 16.1g 5% DV; fat 8.3g 13% DV; cholesterol 172.6mg 58% DV; sodium 1089.7mg 44% DV.

Pork Tofu with Watercress and Bean Sprouts

Prep: 20 mins **Cook:** 1 hr **Total:** 1 hr 20 mins **Servings:** 8 **Yield:** 8 servings

Ingredients
- 1 (2 pound) boneless pork loin, cut into 1/2 inch strips
- 1 cup soy sauce
- ¾ cup water
- 1 teaspoon minced fresh ginger root
- 1 tablespoon coarsely ground black pepper
- 2 bunches watercress - rinsed, dried, cut into 1/2 inch lengths, thick stems discarded
- 8 ounces bean sprouts
- 1 (16 ounce) package firm tofu, drained and cubed

Directions

- **Step 1**
Place pork in a wok or skillet over medium heat. Cook and stir until pork is browned on all sides, about 5 minutes. Stir in the soy sauce, water, ginger, and black pepper; bring to a boil over medium-high heat. Reduce heat to medium, cover, and simmer until meat is tender, about 40 minutes.
- **Step 2**
Stir in the watercress and bean sprouts, and continue to simmer until tender yet still crisp, about 10 minutes more. Mix in the tofu, cover, and simmer 5 minutes more.

Nutrition Facts
Per Serving:
244.7 calories; protein 27.2g 55% DV; carbohydrates 6.5g 2% DV; fat 12.7g 20% DV; cholesterol 55.2mg 18% DV; sodium 1875.9mg 75% DV.

Dol Sot Bi Bim Bap

Prep: 1 hr **Cook:** 1 hr **Total:** 2 hrs **Servings:** 6 **Yield:** 6 servings

Ingredients
- ½ cup soy sauce
- ½ cup white sugar
- ½ cup brown sugar
- ¼ cup minced garlic
- ⅓ cup chopped green onion
- 4 tablespoons toasted sesame seeds
- 20 ounces rib-eye steak, sliced thin
- 1 pinch salt and pepper to taste
- 3 cups uncooked glutinous (sticky) white rice, rinsed
- 6 ½ cups water
- 4 mushrooms dried shiitake mushrooms
- 1 pound fresh spinach, washed and chopped
- 12 ounces cucumber, julienned
- 12 ounces carrots, julienned
- 2 tablespoons sesame oil
- 8 ounces fresh bean sprouts
- 6 large eggs eggs
- 6 sheets nori, crumbled
- 6 tablespoons sesame oil

- ¼ cup chili bean paste (Kochujang)

Directions

- **Step 1**

    Make the marinade for the beef. Combine the soy sauce, sugars, garlic, green onions, sesame seeds in a large bowl; add the sliced beef strips to the marinade, and season with salt and pepper. Cover, and refrigerate for at least 2 hours.

- **Step 2**

    Bring the rice and water to a boil in a saucepan over high heat. Reduce heat to medium-low and cover; simmer until the rice is tender and the liquid has been absorbed, 20 to 25 minutes.

- **Step 3**

    Preheat an oven to 425 degrees F (220 degrees C), and place 6 Korean stone bowls in oven. Combine shiitake mushrooms and 1/2 cup hot water in a small bowl, and soak for about 10 minutes, until pliable. Trim off and discard the stems. Thinly slice the caps. Set aside.

- **Step 4**

    Bring a saucepan of water to a boil. Add spinach to the water just long enough to wilt the leaves, and then drain and pat dry. Set aside. Combine cucumber and carrots in a bowl, and season with salt and pepper. Set aside.

- **Step 5**

    Preheat wok over medium-high heat. Cook carrots and cucumbers in a small amount of sesame oil to soften, stirring frequently. Remove from pan, and set aside. Add a small amount of sesame oil to the pan, and cook spinach in sesame oil for a minute or two. Remove spinach from pan, and set aside. Add the meat strips and marinade to the wok; cook, stirring frequently, until the liquid reduces in volume, about 4 to 5 minutes.

- **Step 6**

    Transfer the stone bowls from the oven to suitable heat resistant surface. Brush each bowl with sesame oil to coat. Divide the rice into the bowls, and gently pack to the bottom (the rice should sizzle as you arrange). Arrange the cucumbers and carrots, bean sprouts, greens, shiitake mushrooms, and beef mixture over each potion of rice. Immediately before serving , add one raw egg yolk to each bowl, drizzle with about a tablespoon of sesame oil, and top with the nori. Serve Kochujang sauce as a condiment.

Cook's Notes:

You can substitute zucchini for the cucumber.

For Dol Sot Bi Bim Bap, you can either fry the egg and place on top, or just add the raw egg yolk on top immediately before serving to allow the person eating to mix it in.

Nutrition Facts

Per Serving:

936.9 calories; protein 35.8g 72% DV; carbohydrates 120.8g 39% DV; fat 37.6g 58% DV; cholesterol 219.9mg 73% DV; sodium 1517.1mg 61% DV.

Sesame Pepper Stir Fry

Prep: 20 mins **Cook:** 15 mins **Total:** 35 mins **Servings:** 8 **Yield:** 8 servings

Ingredients

- 1 small head cabbage, thinly sliced
- 2 eaches red bell peppers, thinly sliced
- 1 onion, sliced
- 8 cloves garlic, finely diced
- 4 teaspoons grated fresh ginger
- ½ cup sesame oil, divided
- 1 pound beef tenderloin, thinly sliced
- ¼ cup soy sauce
- 2 teaspoons white sugar
- 1 teaspoon ground black pepper
- 1 cup water
- 4 teaspoons cornstarch

Directions

- **Step 1**

  Mix cabbage and red bell peppers together in a bowl. Mix onion, garlic, and ginger together in a separate bowl.

- **Step 2**

  Heat a wok or large skillet over medium-high heat; add 1/4 cup sesame oil. Cook and stir beef and onion mixture in the hot oil until beef is browned on both sides, 3 to 4 minutes. Add cabbage mixture to beef mixture; cook, stirring quickly, until cabbage wilts, onion begins to brown, and beef is fully cooked, about 5 minutes.

- **Step 3**

  Stir remaining 1/4 cup sesame oil, soy sauce, sugar, and black pepper into beef and cabbage mixture; toss to coat. Mix water and cornstarch together in a bowl until cornstarch is dissolved; pour into beef and cabbage mixture. Cook and stir until sauce reduces and thickens, about 5 minutes.

Cook's Note:

Beef slices easily against the grain if semi-frozen.

Nutrition Facts

Per Serving:

306 calories; protein 18.1g 36% DV; carbohydrates 13.8g 5% DV; fat 20.2g 31% DV; cholesterol 47.6mg 16% DV; sodium 502.8mg 20% DV.

Charred and Herbed Corn Salad with Crab

Prep: 20 mins **Cook:** 5 mins **Total:** 25 mins **Servings:** 6 **Yield:** 6 servings

Ingredients

- 4 ears corn, kernels cut from cob
- 2 leeks leeks, white parts only, thinly sliced
- 2 cloves garlic, minced
- 2 avocado, NS as to Florida or Californias avocados - peeled, pitted, and diced into 1-inch chunks
- ½ lemon, juiced
- 5 tablespoons vegetable oil
- 1 tablespoon rice vinegar
- 1 tablespoon chopped fresh basil
- 1 teaspoon salt
- ½ teaspoon chopped fresh tarragon
- 2 (6 ounce) cans lump crabmeat, drained and flaked

Directions

- **Step 1**

  Place corn kernels in a colander to filter out small pieces; transfer to a bowl. Add leeks and garlic; stir to combine.

- **Step 2**

  Toss diced avocado with lemon juice in a separate bowl to avoid browning.

- **Step 3**

  Heat vegetable oil in a wok over high heat; cook and stir corn mixture until corn is uniformly browned, 4 to 8 minutes.

- **Step 4**

  Fold corn mixture, avocado, rice vinegar, basil, salt, and tarragon together in a serving bowl. Sprinkle with crabmeat.

Nutrition Facts

Per Serving:

321.8 calories; protein 13.2g 26% DV; carbohydrates 22.6g 7% DV; fat 22.5g 35% DV; cholesterol 30.8mg 10% DV; sodium 566.9mg 23% DV.

Pad Thai with Tofu

Prep: 20 mins **Cook:** 15 mins **Additional:** 10 mins **Total:** 45 mins **Servings:** 4 **Yield:** 4 main-dish servings

Ingredients

- 1 (12 ounce) package tofu, drained and cubed
- 1 tablespoon cornstarch
- 3 tablespoons vegetable oil, divided
- 8 ounces dry rice stick noodles

Sauce:

- ¼ cup water
- ¼ cup sriracha hot sauce
- ¼ cup soy sauce
- 2 tablespoons white sugar
- 1 tablespoon tamarind concentrate
- 1 teaspoon red pepper flakes
- ½ onion, sliced
- 1 egg
- 2 tablespoons chopped spring onions
- 1 tablespoon crushed peanuts
- 1 lime, cut into wedges

Directions

- **Step 1**

Coat tofu with cornstarch in a bowl. Heat 2 tablespoons vegetable oil in a wok or large skillet over medium heat; fry tofu until lightly browned on all sides, 1 to 2 minutes per side.

- **Step 2**

Place noodles in a bowl and pour in enough boiling water to cover; soak until softened, about 3 minutes. Drain.

- **Step 3**

Combine water, sriracha, soy sauce, sugar, tamarind concentrate, and red pepper flakes in a saucepan over low heat. Cook and stir sauce until flavors blend, about 5 minutes.

- **Step 4**

Heat 1 tablespoon vegetable oil in a wok over medium-high heat. Add tofu, noodles, and sliced onion; cook and stir until tofu is golden brown; about 3 minutes. Stir in sauce gradually until noodles are well-coated.

- **Step 5**

Push noodle mixture to one side of the wok. Crack egg onto opposite side of wok; stir until beginning to set, 30 seconds to 1 minute. Stir egg into noodles gently. Garnish with green onions, peanuts, and lime wedges.

Nutrition Facts
Per Serving:

451.8 calories; protein 14.4g 29% DV; carbohydrates 61.1g 20% DV; fat 16.8g 26% DV; cholesterol 46.5mg 16% DV; sodium 1579.2mg 63% DV.

Sichuan Pork Stir-Fry

Prep: 30 mins **Cook:** 10 mins **Additional:** 5 mins **Total:** 45 mins **Servings:** 2 **Yield:** 2 servings

Ingredients

- 6 leaves stem lettuce (celtuce), cut into 1/2-inch pieces
- 1 pinch salt
- 2 teaspoons water
- 1 teaspoon cornstarch
- ½ pound lean pork, cut into 1/2-inch cubes
- 1 teaspoon rice wine (sake)
- ¼ teaspoon salt
- 2 tablespoons chicken stock
- 2 teaspoons soy sauce
- ½ teaspoon Chinese black vinegar
- ½ teaspoon white sugar
- 3 ½ tablespoons vegetable oil
- 1 tablespoon finely chopped pickled red chile peppers
- 2 teaspoons chili bean sauce ((toban djan), such as Lee Kum Kee®)
- 3 eaches spring onions, diced
- 2 cloves garlic, sliced
- 1 (1/2 inch) piece fresh ginger, sliced

Directions

- **Step 1**

Combine stem lettuce and pinch of salt in another bowl.

- **Step 2**

Combine water and cornstarch in a small bowl; stir into a smooth paste.

- **Step 3**

Transfer half of the cornstarch paste into a larger bowl. Add pork, rice wine, and 1/4 teaspoon salt. Mix well and let marinate, about 5 minutes.

- **Step 4**

Whisk remaining cornstarch paste, chicken stock, soy sauce, black vinegar, and sugar in another bowl to make sauce.

- **Step 5**

Heat oil in a wok or large skillet over high heat. Add pork with marinade; cook and stir until browned, 3 to 4 minutes. Stir in pickled chile peppers and chili bean sauce; cook until oil turns red, about 1 minute. Add spring onions, garlic, and ginger; cook and stir until fragrant, about 1 minute. Stir in lettuce; saute until tender, 2 to 3 minutes. Pour in sauce and toss until thickened, about 3 minutes.

Cook's Notes:

Substitute cucumbers for the stem lettuce (celtuce) if desired.

Substitute water for the chicken stock if desired.

Nutrition Facts

Per Serving:

347.2 calories; protein 19.8g 40% DV; carbohydrates 8.3g 3% DV; fat 26.4g 41% DV; cholesterol 49mg 16% DV; sodium 1094.6mg 44% DV.

Singapore Beef Stir-Fry

Prep: 15 mins **Cook:** 20 mins **Additional:** 15 mins **Total:** 50 mins **Servings:** 4 **Yield:** 4 servings

Ingredients

- 6 eaches green onions, green and white parts chopped and separated
- 1 red chile pepper, finely chopped
- 1 green chile pepper, finely chopped
- 2 cloves garlic, chopped
- 3 tablespoons dark soy sauce
- 4 tablespoons walnut oil, divided
- 1 teaspoon dark brown sugar
- 1 pound beef sirloin steak, cut into thin strips
- 8 ounces dried Chinese egg noodles
- 1 (10 ounce) package frozen chopped spinach, thawed and drained
- 1 red bell pepper, chopped
- 1 cup halved snow peas
- ¾ cup halved baby corn
- 1 teaspoon soy sauce, divided, or to taste
- 2 tablespoons sesame seeds

Directions

- **Step 1**

  Combine white parts of the green onions, red chile pepper, green chile pepper, and garlic in a large bowl. Add dark soy sauce, 3 tablespoons walnut oil, and brown sugar; mix marinade well. Add beef to marinade, cover, and refrigerate for a minimum of 15 minutes and up to 24 hours.

- **Step 2**

Bring a large pot of salted water to a boil. Add egg noodles; cook until softened but still firm to the touch, 2 to 3 minutes. Drain.

- **Step 3**

Cook spinach in a separate pot of boiling, lightly salted water until wilted, 3 to 5 minutes. Drain and set aside.

- **Step 4**

Heat 1 teaspoon walnut oil in a wok. Add green parts of the green onions, bell pepper, snow peas, baby corn, and 1/2 teaspoon soy sauce. Stir-fry until lightly browned, yet still crisp, 2 to 3 minutes. Remove from the wok.

- **Step 5**

Stir-fry noodles, 1 teaspoon oil, and 1/2 teaspoon soy sauce in the same wok until crisp, 1 to 2 minutes. Transfer to a plate.

- **Step 6**

Heat 1 teaspoon oil in the wok and stir-fry marinated beef and some of the sesame seeds in batches until fully cooked, 3 to 4 minutes. Add cooked vegetables back to the wok and stir-fry until heated through, about 2 minutes.

- **Step 7**

Place a light layer of drained spinach over the noodles and pour stir-fry mixture on top.

Cook's Note:

I use the spinach water to boil the noodles to retain as much iron as possible.

Nutrition Facts

Per Serving:

516 calories; protein 30.4g 61% DV; carbohydrates 38.5g 12% DV; fat 27.7g 43% DV; cholesterol 117.7mg 39% DV; sodium 1127.4mg 45% DV.

Chicken Singapore Noodles

Prep: 25 mins **Cook:** 10 mins **Additional:** 10 mins **Total:** 45 mins **Servings:** 6 **Yield:** 6 servings

Ingredients

- 6 eaches dry Chinese egg noodle nests
- ¼ cup peanut oil
- 6 cloves garlic, minced
- 2 tablespoons slivered fresh ginger
- 2 teaspoons crushed red pepper flakes
- 1 pound skinless, boneless chicken breast halves
- ⅓ cup green onions, chopped
- ⅔ cup julienned carrot
- 1 (8 ounce) can sliced water chestnuts, drained

- 2 (15 ounce) cans whole straw mushrooms, drained
- ¼ cup peanut butter
- ¼ cup oyster sauce
- 3 tablespoons curry powder
- 2 teaspoons soy sauce

Directions

- **Step 1**

Bring a large pot of lightly-salted water to a rolling boil; add the egg noodle nests and return to a boil. Turn off the heat and let stand for 5 minutes; drain and set aside.

- **Step 2**

Heat the peanut oil in a wok over high heat. Stir in the garlic, ginger, and red pepper flakes; cook a few seconds until the garlic begins to turn golden. Add the chicken, green onions, and carrots. Cook and stir until the chicken is no longer pink, about 5 minutes. Stir in the water chestnuts, mushrooms, peanut butter, oyster sauce, curry powder, and soy sauce until the peanut butter has dissolved into the sauce.

- **Step 3**

Stir the noodles into the chicken mixture; cover and reduce heat to warm or very low. Let stand 10 to 15 minutes for the noodles to absorb some of the sauce.

Nutrition Facts

Per Serving:

412.7 calories; protein 27.6g 55% DV; carbohydrates 41.9g 14% DV; fat 18.3g 28% DV; cholesterol 39mg 13% DV; sodium 814.8mg 33% DV.

Snappy Chicken Stir-Fry

Total Time Prep/Total Time: 30 min Makes 4 servings

Ingredients

- 3 tablespoons cornstarch
- 1-1/2 cups reduced-sodium chicken broth
- 3 tablespoons reduced-sodium soy sauce
- 3/4 teaspoon garlic powder
- 3/4 teaspoon ground ginger
- 1/4 teaspoon crushed red pepper flakes
- 1 package (16 ounces) frozen sugar snap stir-fry vegetable blend
- 1 tablespoon sesame or canola oil
- 2 cups cubed cooked chicken breast
- 2 cups hot cooked brown rice
- 1/4 cup sliced almonds, toasted

Directions

- In a small bowl, combine the cornstarch, broth, soy sauce, garlic powder, ginger and pepper flakes; set aside.
- In a large skillet or wok, stir-fry vegetable blend in oil for 5-7 minutes or until vegetables are tender.
- Stir cornstarch mixture and add to the pan. Bring to a boil; cook and stir for 2 minutes or until thickened. Add chicken; heat through. Serve with rice; sprinkle with almonds.

Asparagus Turkey Stir-Fry

Total Time Prep/Total Time: 20 min. Makes 4 servings

Ingredients

- 2 teaspoons cornstarch
- 1/4 cup chicken broth
- 1 tablespoon lemon juice
- 1 teaspoon soy sauce
- 1 pound turkey breast tenderloins, cut into 1/2-inch strips
- 1 garlic clove, minced
- 2 tablespoons canola oil, divided
- 1 pound fresh asparagus, trimmed and cut into 1-1/2-inch pieces
- 1 jar (2 ounces) sliced pimientos, drained

Directions

- In a small bowl, combine the cornstarch, broth, lemon juice and soy sauce until smooth; set aside. In a large skillet or wok, stir-fry turkey and garlic in 1 tablespoon oil until meat is no longer pink; remove and keep warm.
- Stir-fry asparagus in remaining oil until crisp-tender. Add pimientos. Stir broth mixture and add to the pan; cook and stir for 1 minute or until thickened. Return turkey to the pan; heat through.

Nutrition Facts

1-1/4 cups: 205 calories, 9g fat (1g saturated fat), 56mg cholesterol, 204mg sodium, 5g carbohydrate (1g sugars, 1g fiber), 28g protein. **Diabetic Exchanges:** 3 lean meat, 1-1/2 fat, 1 vegetable.

Coconut Curry Shrimp

Total Time Prep/Total Time: 25 min. Makes 3 servings

Ingredients

- 2/3 cup coconut milk
- 1 tablespoon fish sauce
- 1-1/2 teaspoons curry powder
- 1 teaspoon brown sugar
- 1/4 teaspoon salt
- 1/4 teaspoon pepper

- 1 pound uncooked large shrimp, peeled and deveined
- 1 medium sweet red pepper, finely chopped
- 2 green onions, chopped
- 1/4 cup minced fresh cilantro
- Hot cooked jasmine rice
- Lime wedges

Directions

- In a small bowl, combine the first six ingredients. In a large skillet or wok, stir-fry shrimp in 2 tablespoons coconut milk mixture until shrimp turn pink. Remove and keep warm.
- Add the red pepper, onions and remaining coconut milk mixture to pan. Bring to a boil; cook and stir for 3-4 minutes or until vegetables are crisp-tender. Add shrimp and cilantro; heat through. Serve with rice and lime wedges.

Nutrition Facts

1 cup (calculated without rice): 256 calories, 13g fat (10g saturated fat), 184mg cholesterol, 841mg sodium, 8g carbohydrate (4g sugars, 2g fiber), 27g protein.

Thai Shrimp Stir-Fry

Total Time Prep: 15 min. Cook: 10 min. Makes 4 servings

Ingredients

- 2 medium sweet red peppers, cut into thin slices
- 1 teaspoon canola oil
- 1 cup fresh snow peas
- 1/2 cup thinly sliced green onions
- 1 garlic clove, minced
- 1/2 cup reduced-sodium chicken broth
- 2 tablespoons reduced-fat peanut butter
- 4-1/2 teaspoons reduced-sodium soy sauce
- 1 tablespoon rice vinegar
- 1 teaspoon sesame oil
- 1 teaspoon minced fresh gingerroot
- 1/2 teaspoon crushed red pepper flakes
- 1 pound uncooked medium shrimp, peeled and deveined
- Hot cooked fettuccine

Directions

- In a large nonstick skillet or wok, stir-fry red peppers in hot canola oil for 1 minute. Add the snow peas, green onions and garlic; stir-fry 2-3 minutes longer or until vegetables are crisp-tender. remove and keep warm.
- In the same skillet, combine the broth, peanut butter, soy sauce, vinegar, sesame oil, ginger and pepper flakes. Cook and stir until peanut butter is melted and mixture comes to a boil. Stir in shrimp. Cook and stir for 2 minutes or until shrimp turn pink. Return red pepper mixture to skillet; heat through. Serve over fettuccine.

Nutrition Facts

1 cup: 206 calories, 8g fat (1g saturated fat), 168mg cholesterol, 565mg sodium, 12g carbohydrate (0 sugars, 3g fiber), 22g protein. **Diabetic Exchanges:** 3 lean meat, 1 vegetable, 1 fat, 1/2 starch.

Mandarin Pork Stir-Fry

Total Time Prep/Total Time: 25 min. Makes 4 servings

Ingredients

- 2 cups uncooked instant rice
- 1 tablespoon cornstarch
- 1/2 teaspoon garlic powder
- 1/2 teaspoon ground ginger
- 1/2 cup orange juice
- 1/4 cup water
- 2 tablespoons soy sauce
- 1 pork tenderloin (1 pound), cut into 2-inch strips
- 2 tablespoons canola oil
- 1 package (14 ounces) frozen sugar snap peas
- 1 can (11 ounces) mandarin oranges, drained

Directions

- Cook rice according to package directions. Meanwhile, in a small bowl, combine the cornstarch, garlic powder and ginger. Stir in orange juice until smooth. Stir in water and soy sauce; set aside.
- In a large wok or skillet, stir-fry pork in oil until juices run clear; remove to a platter and keep warm. In the same skillet, stir-fry peas until tender. Return pork to skillet. Stir orange juice mixture; add to skillet. Cook and stir for 2 minutes or until thickened. Gently stir in oranges. Serve with rice.

Nutrition Facts

2 cups: 473 calories, 11g fat (2g saturated fat), 63mg cholesterol, 514mg sodium, 61g carbohydrate (14g sugars, 5g fiber), 30g protein.

Asparagus Tofu Stir-Fry

Total Time Prep: 15 min. Cook: 20 min. Makes 4 servings

Ingredients
- 1 tablespoon cornstarch
- 1/2 teaspoon sugar
- 1-1/4 cups vegetable broth
- 4 teaspoons reduced-sodium soy sauce
- 2 teaspoons minced fresh gingerroot, divided
- 3 teaspoons canola oil, divided
- 1 pound fresh asparagus, trimmed and cut into 1-inch pieces
- 1 medium yellow summer squash, halved and sliced
- 2 green onions, thinly sliced
- 1 package (14 ounces) extra-firm tofu, drained and cut into 1/2-inch cubes
- 1/4 teaspoon salt
- 1/4 teaspoon pepper
- 2 cups hot cooked brown rice
- 2 tablespoons sliced almonds, toasted

Directions
- In a small bowl, combine the cornstarch, sugar, broth and soy sauce until smooth; set aside.
- In a large nonstick skillet or wok, stir-fry 1 teaspoon ginger in 1 teaspoon oil for 1 minute. Add asparagus; stir-fry for 2 minutes. Add squash; stir-fry 2 minutes longer. Add onions; stir-fry 1 minute longer or until vegetables are crisp-tender. Remove and keep warm.
- In the same pan, stir-fry tofu, salt, pepper and remaining ginger in remaining oil for 7-9 minutes or until lightly browned. Remove and keep warm.
- Stir cornstarch mixture and add to the pan. Bring to a boil; cook and stir for 2 minutes or until thickened. Add asparagus mixture and tofu; heat through. Serve with rice; sprinkle with almonds.

Nutrition Facts

1 cup: 278 calories, 11g fat (1g saturated fat), 0 cholesterol, 682mg sodium, 34g carbohydrate (4g sugars, 4g fiber), 14g protein. **Diabetic Exchanges:** 2 starch, 1 lean meat, 1 vegetable, 1 fat.

Spicy Chicken Lettuce Wraps

Total Time Prep/Total Time: 30 min. Makes 4 servings

Ingredients
- 1 pound chicken tenderloins, cut into 1/2-inch pieces
- 1/8 teaspoon pepper
- 2 tablespoons canola oil, divided

- 1 medium onion, finely chopped
- 1 small green pepper, finely chopped
- 1 small sweet red pepper, finely chopped
- 1 can (8 ounces) sliced water chestnuts, drained and finely chopped
- 1 can (4 ounces) mushroom stems and pieces, drained and finely chopped
- 2 garlic cloves, minced
- 1/3 cup stir-fry sauce
- 1 teaspoon reduced-sodium soy sauce
- 8 Bibb or Boston lettuce leaves
- 1/4 cup salted peanuts
- 2 teaspoons minced fresh cilantro

Directions

- Sprinkle chicken with pepper. In a large skillet or wok, stir-fry chicken in 1 tablespoon oil until no longer pink. Remove and set aside.
- Stir-fry onion and peppers in remaining oil for 5 minutes. Add the water chestnuts, mushrooms and garlic; stir-fry 2-3 minutes longer or until vegetables are crisp-tender. Add stir-fry sauce and soy sauce. Stir in chicken; heat through.
- Place 1/2 cup chicken mixture on each lettuce leaf; sprinkle each with 1-1/2 teaspoons peanuts and 1/4 teaspoon cilantro. Fold lettuce over filling.

Nutrition Facts

2 each: 303 calories, 12g fat (1g saturated fat), 67mg cholesterol, 981mg sodium, 20g carbohydrate (7g sugars, 4g fiber), 32g protein.

Thai-Style Brisket

Total Time Prep: 1 hour Cook: 8-1/2 hours Makes 8 servings

Ingredients

- 1 fresh beef brisket (3 to 4 pounds), cut in half
- 3 tablespoons olive oil, divided
- 1 cup chunky peanut butter
- 2/3 cup soy sauce
- 4 teaspoons sesame oil
- 1 tablespoon minced fresh cilantro
- 1 tablespoon lemon juice

- 1 teaspoon garlic powder
- 1 teaspoon crushed red pepper flakes
- 1 teaspoon pepper
- 1 tablespoon cornstarch
- 1 cup water
- 1-1/4 cups julienned carrots
- 1 medium sweet red pepper, sliced
- 1 medium green pepper, sliced
- 1/2 cup chopped green onions
- 1 cup unsalted peanuts, optional
- Hot cooked rice

Directions

- In a large skillet over medium-high heat, brown brisket on both sides in 2 tablespoons olive oil. Transfer meat and drippings to a 5-qt. slow cooker. Combine the peanut butter, soy sauce, sesame oil, cilantro, lemon juice, garlic, pepper flakes and pepper; pour over brisket. Cover and cook on low for 8-9 hours or until meat is tender.
- Remove brisket and keep warm. Combine cornstarch and water until smooth; stir into cooking juices. Cover and cook on high for 30 minutes or until thickened. Meanwhile, in a large skillet or wok, stir-fry the carrots, peppers and onions in remaining olive oil until crisp-tender. Add peanuts if desired. Stir cooking juices and stir into vegetable mixture.
- Thinly slice meat across the grain. Place rice on a large serving platter; top with meat and vegetable mixture.

Nutrition Facts

1 each: 505 calories, 31g fat (6g saturated fat), 72mg cholesterol, 1455mg sodium, 12g carbohydrate (5g sugars, 4g fiber), 46g protein.

Pork 'n' Pea Pod Stir-Fry

Total Time Prep: 10 min. + marinating Cook: 15 min. Makes 3 servings

Ingredients

- 2 tablespoons reduced-sodium soy sauce
- 2 tablespoons honey
- 1-1/2 teaspoons minced fresh gingerroot
- 1/2 to 1 teaspoon crushed red pepper flakes
- 3/4 pound pork tenderloin, cut into 2-inch strips
- 2 teaspoons canola oil
- 1 tablespoon cornstarch

- 1/3 cup orange juice
- 2 tablespoons cider vinegar
- 1 pound fresh snow peas
- 2 teaspoons minced garlic
- 1 teaspoon grated orange zest

Directions

- In a small bowl, combine the soy sauce, honey, ginger and pepper flakes. Place 3 tablespoons in a large bowl; add the pork and turn to coat. Cover; refrigerate for 1 hour. Cover and refrigerate remaining marinade.
- Combine the cornstarch, orange juice, vinegar and reserved marinade; stir until blended and set aside. Drain and discard marinade from pork. In a large nonstick skillet or wok, stir-fry pork in oil for 4-5 minutes or until no longer pink. Remove pork and keep warm.
- In the same pan, stir-fry snow peas for 2-3 minutes or until crisp-tender. Stir in garlic and orange zest. Stir cornstarch mixture and stir into pan. Bring to a boil; cook and stir for 1-2 minutes or until thickened. Return pork to the pan; heat through.

Nutrition Facts

1-1/3 cups: 286 calories, 7g fat (2g saturated fat), 63mg cholesterol, 354mg sodium, 26g carbohydrate (16g sugars, 4g fiber), 28g protein. **Diabetic Exchanges:** 3 lean meat, 2 vegetable, 1 starch, 1/2 fat.

Balsamic Pork Stir-Fry

Total Time Prep/Total Time: 30 min. Makes 5 servings

Ingredients

- 1 pork tenderloin (1 pound), cut into thin strips
- 2/3 cup balsamic vinaigrette, divided
- 1-1/2 cups sliced fresh carrots
- 1 cup sliced fresh mushrooms
- 1 can (8 ounces) sliced water chestnuts, drained
- 2 tablespoons hoisin sauce
- Hot cooked rice

Directions

- In a large skillet or wok, stir-fry pork in 2 tablespoons vinaigrette for 3-4 minutes or until browned. Remove and keep warm.
- Stir-fry carrots in 2 tablespoons vinaigrette for 2 minutes. Add mushrooms; stir-fry 2 minutes longer. Add water chestnuts and stir-fry 2-3 minutes longer or until vegetables are crisp-tender. Add hoisin sauce and remaining vinaigrette. Bring to a boil; cook for 1 minute. Add pork and heat through. Serve with rice.

Stir-Fried Scallops and Asparagus

Total Time Prep/Total Time: 25 min. Makes 4 servings

Ingredients
- 1 package (3 ounces) chicken ramen noodles
- 1 pound fresh asparagus, trimmed and cut into 1-inch pieces
- 1 medium sweet red pepper, julienned
- 1 tablespoon olive oil
- 3 green onions, thinly sliced
- 1 garlic clove, minced
- 1 pound sea scallops, halved horizontally
- 1 tablespoon lime juice
- 2 tablespoons reduced-sodium soy sauce
- 1 teaspoon sesame oil
- 1/4 to 1 teaspoon hot pepper sauce

Directions
- Discard seasoning package from ramen noodles or save for another use. Cook ramen noodles according to package directions; keep warm.
- Meanwhile, in a nonstick skillet or wok, stir-fry asparagus and red pepper in oil for 2 minutes or until vegetables are crisp-tender. Add green onions and garlic, stir-fry 1 minute longer. Stir in scallops. Stir-fry for 3 minutes or until scallops are firm and opaque.
- Combine the lime juice, soy sauce, sesame oil and hot pepper sauce; stir into skillet. Serve with ramen noodles.

Nutrition Facts
1 cup: 269 calories, 9g fat (3g saturated fat), 37mg cholesterol, 578mg sodium, 22g carbohydrate (2g sugars, 2g fiber), 24g protein. **Diabetic Exchanges:** 3 lean meat, 1 starch, 1 vegetable, 1 fat.

Mexican Fiesta Steak Stir-Fry

Total Time Prep/Total Time: 30 min. Makes 4 servings

Ingredients
- 1 pound boneless beef top loin steak, trimmed and cut into thin strips
- 3 garlic cloves, minced
- 1 to 2 tablespoons canola oil
- 1 package (14 ounces) frozen pepper strips, thawed
- 1-1/3 cups chopped sweet onion
- 2 plum tomatoes, chopped

- 1 can (4 ounces) chopped green chilies
- 1/2 teaspoon salt
- 1/2 teaspoon dried oregano
- 1/4 teaspoon pepper
- Hot cooked rice

Directions

In a large skillet or wok, stir-fry beef and garlic in oil until meat is no longer pink. Remove and keep warm. Add peppers and onion to pan; stir-fry until tender. Stir in the tomatoes, chilies, salt, oregano, pepper and beef; heat through. Serve with rice.

Nutrition Facts

1-1/2 cups (calculated without rice): 247 calories, 9g fat (2g saturated fat), 50mg cholesterol, 473mg sodium, 13g carbohydrate (7g sugars, 3g fiber), 26g protein. **Diabetic Exchanges:** 3 lean meat, 2 vegetable, 1 fat.

Sugar Snap Pea Stir-Fry

Total Time Prep/Total Time: 20 min. Makes 6 servings

Ingredients

- 1 pound fresh sugar snap peas
- 2 teaspoons canola oil
- 1 garlic clove, minced
- 2 teaspoons minced fresh gingerroot
- 1-1/2 teaspoons balsamic vinegar
- 1-1/2 teaspoons reduced-sodium soy sauce
- 1 teaspoon sesame oil
- Dash cayenne pepper
- 1 tablespoon minced fresh basil or 1 teaspoon dried basil
- 2 teaspoons sesame seeds, toasted

Directions

- In a large nonstick skillet or wok, saute the peas in canola oil until crisp-tender. Add the garlic, ginger, vinegar, soy sauce, sesame oil and cayenne; saute 1 minute longer. Add basil; toss to combine. Sprinkle with sesame seeds.

Nutrition Facts

1/2 cup: 60 calories, 3g fat (0 saturated fat), 0 cholesterol, 59mg sodium, 6g carbohydrate (3g sugars, 2g fiber), 3g protein. **Diabetic Exchanges:** 1 vegetable, 1/2 fat.

Beef Orange Stir-Fry

Total Time Prep/Total Time: 25 min. Makes 2 servings

Ingredients
- 1 tablespoon cornstarch
- 1/4 cup cold water
- 1/4 cup orange juice
- 1 tablespoon reduced-sodium soy sauce
- 1/2 teaspoon sesame oil
- Dash crushed red pepper flakes
- 1/2 pound boneless beef sirloin steak, cut into thin strips
- 2 teaspoons canola oil, divided
- 3 cups frozen sugar snap stir-fry vegetable blend, thawed
- 1 garlic clove, minced
- 1 cup hot cooked rice

Directions
- In a small bowl, combine the first 6 ingredients until smooth; set aside.
- In a large skillet or wok, stir-fry beef in 1 teaspoon oil until no longer pink, 3-4 minutes. Remove with a slotted spoon and keep warm.
- Stir-fry vegetable blend and garlic in remaining oil for 3 minutes. Stir cornstarch mixture and add to the pan. Bring to a boil; cook and stir until thickened, about 2 minutes. Add beef; heat through. Serve with rice.

Nutrition Facts

1-1/2 cups with 1/2 cup rice: 390 calories, 11g fat (3g saturated fat), 64mg cholesterol, 396mg sodium, 41g carbohydrate (3g sugars, 3g fiber), 26g protein. **Diabetic Exchanges:** 3 lean meat, 2 starch, 2 vegetable, 1 fat.

Sizzling Chicken Lo Mein

Total Time Prep/Total Time: 30 min. Makes 4 servings

Ingredients
- 8 ounces uncooked linguine
- 3/4 pound boneless skinless chicken breasts, cubed
- 2 tablespoons olive oil
- 5 tablespoons stir-fry sauce, divided

- 4 tablespoons teriyaki sauce, divided
- 1 package (12 ounces) frozen stir-fry vegetable blend

Directions
- Cook linguine according to package directions. Meanwhile, in a large skillet or wok, stir-fry chicken in oil until no longer pink. Add 2 tablespoons each stir fry sauce and teriyaki sauce. Remove chicken from pan.
- Stir-fry vegetables and 1 tablespoon each stir-fry sauce and teriyaki sauce in the same pan for 4-6 minutes or until vegetables are crisp-tender. Drain linguine. Add the linguine, chicken and remaining sauces to the pan; stir-fry for 2-3 minutes or until heated through.

Chicken Soba Noodle Toss

Total Time Prep/Total Time: 30 min. Makes 4 servings

Ingredients
- 2 teaspoons cornstarch
- 1/2 cup reduced-sodium chicken broth
- 2 tablespoons brown sugar
- 3 garlic cloves, minced
- 1 tablespoon butter, melted
- 1 tablespoon reduced-sodium soy sauce
- 1 tablespoon hoisin sauce
- 2 teaspoons minced fresh gingerroot
- 2 teaspoons rice vinegar
- 1/4 teaspoon pepper
- 6 ounces uncooked Japanese soba noodles
- 3/4 pound chicken tenderloins, cubed
- 4 teaspoons canola oil, divided
- 3 cups fresh broccoli stir-fry blend
- 1/4 cup chopped unsalted cashews

Directions
- In a small bowl, combine the first 10 ingredients until blended; set aside.
- Cook noodles according to package directions. Meanwhile, in a large skillet or wok, stir-fry chicken in 2 teaspoons oil until no longer pink. Remove and keep warm.
- Stir-fry broccoli blend in remaining oil for 4-6 minutes or until vegetables are crisp-tender.
- Stir cornstarch mixture and add to the pan. Bring to a boil; cook and stir for 2 minutes or until thickened. Drain noodles; add to pan. Add chicken; heat through. Sprinkle with cashews.

Nutrition Facts

1-1/2 cups: 417 calories, 12g fat (3g saturated fat), 58mg cholesterol, 715mg sodium, 52g carbohydrate (11g sugars, 2g fiber), 30g protein.

Peking Shrimp

Total Time Prep/Total Time: 25 min. Makes 4 servings

Ingredients

- 1 tablespoon cornstarch
- 1/4 cup cold water
- 1/4 cup corn syrup
- 2 tablespoons reduced-sodium soy sauce
- 2 tablespoons sherry or chicken broth
- 1 garlic clove, minced
- 1/4 teaspoon ground ginger
- 1 small green pepper, cut into 1-inch pieces
- 2 tablespoons canola oil
- 1 pound uncooked medium shrimp, peeled and deveined
- 1 medium tomato, cut into wedges
- Hot cooked rice, optional

Directions

- In a small bowl, combine cornstarch and water until smooth. Stir in the corn syrup, soy sauce, sherry, garlic and ginger; set aside.
- In a nonstick skillet or wok, stir-fry green pepper in oil for 3 minutes. Add shrimp; cook 3 minutes longer or until shrimp turn pink.
- Stir cornstarch mixture and add to the pan. Bring to a boil; cook and stir for 2 minutes or until thickened. Add tomato; heat through. Serve with rice if desired.

Nutrition Facts

3/4 cup (calculated without rice): 237 calories, 8g fat (1g saturated fat), 168mg cholesterol, 532mg sodium, 21g carbohydrate (9g sugars, 1g fiber), 19g protein. **Diabetic Exchanges:** 2 lean meat, 1-1/2 fat, 1 starch, 1 vegetable.

Orange Beef and Asparagus Stir-fry

Total Time Prep/Total Time: 30 min. Makes 4 servings

Ingredients

- 4 teaspoons cornstarch
- 3/4 cup orange juice

- 4 green onions, thinly sliced
- 3 tablespoons reduced-sodium soy sauce
- 3 tablespoons honey
- 2 teaspoons minced fresh gingerroot
- 1 garlic clove, minced
- 2 cups cut fresh asparagus (1-inch pieces)
- 1 medium sweet red pepper, sliced
- 1 cup julienned carrots
- 1 tablespoon canola oil
- 3/4 pound leftover grilled steaks, thinly sliced
- 1/2 cup honey-roasted peanuts
- Hot cooked rice

Directions

- In a small bowl, whisk the cornstarch, orange juice, onions, soy sauce, honey, ginger and garlic until blended; set aside.
- In a large skillet or wok, stir-fry the asparagus, pepper and carrots in oil for 2-3 minutes or until vegetables are crisp-tender.
- Stir cornstarch mixture and add to the pan. Bring to a boil; cook and stir for 2 minutes or until thickened. Add beef; heat through. Sprinkle with peanuts. Serve with rice.

Nutrition Facts

1 cup (calculated without rice): 428 calories, 18g fat (4g saturated fat), 76mg cholesterol, 597mg sodium, 35g carbohydrate (24g sugars, 5g fiber), 33g protein.

Curried Fried Rice with Pineapple

Total Time Prep/Total Time: 30 min. Makes 8 servings

Ingredients

- 4 tablespoons canola oil, divided
- 2 large eggs, beaten
- 1 small onion, finely chopped
- 2 shallots, finely chopped
- 3 garlic cloves, minced
- 4 cups cold cooked rice
- 1 can (8 ounces) unsweetened pineapple chunks, drained
- 1/2 cup lightly salted cashews
- 1/2 cup frozen peas
- 1/3 cup minced fresh cilantro

- 1/4 cup raisins
- 3 tablespoons chicken broth
- 2 tablespoons fish sauce
- 1-1/2 teaspoons curry powder
- 1 teaspoon sugar
- 1/4 teaspoon crushed red pepper flakes

Directions
- In a large skillet or wok, heat 1 tablespoon oil over medium-high heat; add eggs. As eggs set, lift edges, letting uncooked portion flow underneath. When eggs are completely cooked, remove to a plate and keep warm.
- In the same pan, stir-fry onion and shallots in remaining oil until tender. Add garlic; cook 1 minute longer. Stir in the rice, pineapple, cashews, peas, cilantro, raisins, broth, fish sauce, curry, sugar and pepper flakes; heat through. Chop egg into small pieces; add to rice mixture.

Ginger-Peach Pork Skillet

Total Time Prep/Total Time: 25 min. Makes 4 servings

Ingredients
- 1 package (16 ounces) frozen stir-fry vegetable blend
- 1 tablespoon canola oil
- 1/2 cup peach preserves
- 3 tablespoons reduced-sodium teriyaki sauce
- 3/4 teaspoon ground ginger
- 1/4 teaspoon salt
- 1/4 teaspoon garlic powder
- 1/4 teaspoon crushed red pepper flakes
- 1 can (14-1/2 ounces) reduced-sodium chicken broth
- 3 tablespoons cornstarch
- 2 packages (8-1/2 ounces each) ready-to-serve whole grain brown and wild rice medley
- 1 can (8-1/2 ounces) sliced peaches, drained and coarsely chopped
- 2-3/4 cups sliced grilled pork tenderloin

Directions
- Stir-fry vegetable blend in oil in a large skillet or wok, until vegetables are crisp-tender, about 4 minutes. Stir in the preserves, teriyaki sauce, ginger, salt, garlic powder and pepper flakes.
- Whisk broth and cornstarch until smooth. Gradually stir into skillet. Bring to a boil; cook and stir for 2 minutes or until thickened.

- Meanwhile, prepare rice according to package directions. Stir peaches and pork into the skillet and heat through. Serve with rice.

Nutrition Facts

1-1/2 cups: 639 calories, 11g fat (2g saturated fat), 64mg cholesterol, 1603mg sodium, 102g carbohydrate (41g sugars, 6g fiber), 34g protein.

Nutty Chicken Stir-Fry

Total Time Prep: 20 min. Cook: 15 min. Makes 5 servings

Ingredients
- 1 pound boneless skinless chicken breasts, chopped
- 1 tablespoon canola oil
- 1 package (16 ounces) frozen stir-fry vegetable blend
- 6 garlic cloves, minced
- 2 tablespoons brown sugar
- 4 teaspoons cornstarch
- 3/4 teaspoon ground ginger
- 1/2 cup chicken broth
- 1/3 cup reduced-sodium soy sauce
- 1/4 cup chunky peanut butter
- 5 to 6 drops hot pepper sauce
- 3 cups shredded cabbage
- 3/4 cup salted peanuts, chopped
- Hot cooked rice

Directions
- In a large skillet or wok, stir-fry chicken in oil for 2 minutes. Add vegetables; cook 4 minutes longer. Add garlic; stir-fry until chicken is no longer pink and vegetables are crisp-tender.
- In a small bowl, combine the brown sugar, cornstarch and ginger; stir in the broth, soy sauce, peanut butter and pepper sauce until blended. Pour over chicken mixture.
- Bring to a boil; cook and stir for 2 minutes or until thickened. Add cabbage; cook 2 minutes longer or until crisp-tender. Sprinkle with peanuts. Serve with rice.

Nutrition Facts

1-1/4 cups: 434 calories, 22g fat (3g saturated fat), 51mg cholesterol, 991mg sodium, 31g carbohydrate (8g sugars, 7g fiber), 31g protein.

Chicken Chow Mein

Total Time Prep/Total Time: 30 min. Makes 2 servings

Ingredients

- 1 tablespoon cornstarch
- 2/3 cup reduced-sodium chicken broth
- 1 teaspoon reduced-sodium soy sauce
- 1/2 teaspoon salt
- 1/4 teaspoon ground ginger
- 1/4 pound sliced fresh mushrooms
- 2/3 cup thinly sliced celery
- 1/4 cup sliced onion
- 1/4 cup thinly sliced green pepper
- 2 tablespoons julienned carrot
- 1 teaspoon canola oil
- 1 garlic clove, minced
- 1 cup cubed cooked chicken breast
- 1 cup cooked brown rice
- 2 tablespoons chow mein noodles

Directions

- In a small bowl, combine the cornstarch, broth, soy sauce, salt and ginger until smooth; set aside.
- In a large skillet or wok, stir-fry the mushrooms, celery, onion, pepper and carrot in oil for 5 minutes. Add garlic; stir-fry 1-2 minutes longer or until vegetables are crisp-tender.
- Stir cornstarch mixture and add to the pan. Bring to a boil; cook and stir for 2 minutes or until thickened. Add chicken; heat through. Serve with rice; sprinkle with chow mein noodles.

Nutrition Facts

1 cup chow mein with 1/2 cup cooked brown rice and 1 tablespoon chow mein noodles: 307 calories, 7g fat (1g saturated fat), 54mg cholesterol, 984mg sodium, 35g carbohydrate (4g sugars, 4g fiber), 27g protein. **Diabetic Exchanges:** 3 lean meat, 2 starch, 1 vegetable, 1/2 fat.

Shrimp Lo Mein

Total Time Prep: 25 min. Cook: 15 min. Makes 4 servings

Ingredients

- 1 pound uncooked medium shrimp, peeled and deveined
- 2 garlic cloves, sliced
- Dash blackened seasoning
- 6 ounces uncooked whole wheat linguine
- 4 teaspoons cornstarch
- 1/3 cup water

- 1/4 cup ketchup
- 2 tablespoons reduced-sodium soy sauce
- 2 tablespoons sherry or reduced-sodium chicken broth
- 2 teaspoons honey
- 1/4 teaspoon ground ginger
- 1/4 teaspoon crushed red pepper flakes
- 2 tablespoons olive oil, divided
- 1 celery rib, sliced
- 1 medium carrot, chopped
- 1/2 cup sliced fresh mushrooms
- 1/4 cup fresh broccoli florets
- 2 tablespoons chopped cashews
- 1 can (8 ounces) unsweetened pineapple chunks, drained

Directions
- In a small bowl, combine the shrimp, garlic and blackened seasoning; set aside. Cook linguine according to package directions.
- Meanwhile, in a small bowl, combine the cornstarch, water, ketchup, soy sauce, sherry, honey, ginger and pepper flakes until blended; set aside.
- In a large nonstick skillet or wok, stir-fry shrimp in 1 tablespoon oil for 2-3 minutes or until no longer pink. Remove with a slotted spoon and keep warm.
- Stir-fry celery and carrot in remaining oil for 5 minutes. Add the mushrooms, broccoli and cashews; stir-fry 4-6 minutes longer or until vegetables are crisp-tender.
- Stir cornstarch mixture and add to the pan. Bring to a boil; cook and stir for 2 minutes or until thickened. Drain linguine; stir into skillet. Add shrimp and pineapple; heat through.

Nutrition Facts
1 cup: 401 calories, 11g fat (2g saturated fat), 138mg cholesterol, 678mg sodium, 53g carbohydrate (15g sugars, 6g fiber), 25g protein.

Shrimp and Broccoli Stir-Fry

Yield 4 servings (serving size: 1 cup)

Ingredients
- 1/4 cup fat-free, less-sodium chicken broth
- 2 tablespoons rice vinegar
- 2 tablespoons low-sodium soy sauce
- 2 teaspoons cornstarch
- 1/2 teaspoon dark sesame oil

- 1/4 teaspoon crushed red pepper
- 1 tablespoon canola oil, divided
- 1 tablespoon minced peeled fresh ginger
- 1 tablespoon bottled minced garlic
- 1 pound peeled and deveined large shrimp
- 1/4 teaspoon salt
- 4 cups small broccoli florets
- 1 cup vertically sliced onion

How to Make It
- **Step 1**

Combine first 6 ingredients in a small bowl, stirring with a whisk.
- **Step 2**

Heat 2 teaspoons canola oil in a large nonstick skillet over medium-high heat. Add ginger and garlic to pan; stir-fry 30 seconds. Sprinkle shrimp with salt. Add shrimp to pan, and stir-fry 3 minutes or until done. Remove shrimp mixture from the pan.
- **Step 3**

Add remaining 1 teaspoon canola oil to pan. Add broccoli and onion to pan; stir-fry 4 minutes or until broccoli is crisp-tender. Add shrimp mixture and broth mixture to pan; cook 1 minute or until thickened, stirring constantly.

Pork and Vegetable Stir-Fry with Cashew Rice

Yield 4 servings (serving size: 1 1/2 cups pork mixture and 1/2 cup cashew rice)

Ingredients
- 3/4 cup uncooked long-grain rice
- 1/3 cup chopped green onions
- 1/4 cup dry-roasted cashews, salted and coarsely chopped
- 1/2 teaspoon salt
- 2/3 cup fat-free, less-sodium chicken broth
- 2 tablespoons cornstarch, divided
- 3 tablespoons low-sodium soy sauce, divided
- 2 tablespoons honey
- 1 (1-pound) pork tenderloin, trimmed and cut into 1/2-inch cubes
- 1 tablespoon canola oil, divided
- 2 cups sliced mushrooms (about 4 ounces)
- 1 cup chopped onion
- 1 tablespoon grated peeled fresh ginger

- 2 garlic cloves, minced
- 2 cups sugar snap peas, trimmed (about 6 ounces)
- 1 cup chopped red bell pepper (about 1)

How to Make It

- **Step 1**

  Cook the rice according to package directions, omitting salt and fat. Stir in 1/3 cup chopped green onions, chopped dry-roasted cashews, and salt; set aside, and keep warm.

- **Step 2**

  Combine 2/3 cup chicken broth, 1 tablespoon cornstarch, 2 tablespoons low-sodium soy sauce, and honey in a small bowl, and set aside.

- **Step 3**

  Combine pork, remaining 1 tablespoon cornstarch, and the remaining 1 tablespoon soy sauce in a bowl, tossing well to coat. Heat 2 teaspoons oil in a large nonstick skillet over medium-high heat. Add pork; sauté 4 minutes or until browned. Remove from pan.

- **Step 4**

  Add remaining 1 teaspoon oil to pan. Add mushrooms and 1 cup onion; sauté 2 minutes. Stir in ginger and garlic; sauté 30 seconds. Add peas and bell pepper to pan; sauté 1 minute. Stir in pork; sauté 1 minute. Add reserved broth mixture to pan. Bring to a boil; cook 1 minute or until thick, stirring constantly. Serve over cashew rice.

Sweet-Spicy Chicken and Vegetable Stir-Fry

Yield Serves 4 (serving size: 1 cup)

Ingredients

- 3 tablespoons dark brown sugar
- 1 1/2 tablespoons lower-sodium soy sauce
- 1 tablespoon fish sauce
- 1 tablespoon rice vinegar
- 1 tablespoon sambal oelek
- 1 teaspoon dark sesame oil
- 3/4 teaspoon cornstarch
- 2 tablespoons canola oil, divided
- 1 pound skinless, boneless chicken breast, cut into bite-sized pieces
- 8 ounces sugar snap peas
- 1 red bell pepper, sliced
- 1/2 medium red onion, cut into thin wedges
- 1/4 cup sliced green onions
- 1/4 cup unsalted dry-roasted peanuts

How to Make It

- **Step 1**

Combine the first 7 ingredients, stirring well; set aside.

- **Step 2**

Heat a large wok or large heavy skillet over high heat. Add 1 tablespoon canola oil to pan; swirl to coat. Add chicken; stir-fry 4 minutes or until browned and done. Remove chicken from wok. Add remaining 1 tablespoon canola oil to wok; swirl to coat. Add sugar snap peas, bell pepper, and red onion; stir-fry 3 minutes or until vegetables are crisp-tender. Stir in brown sugar mixture; cook 1 minute or until thickened. Stir in chicken; toss to coat. Sprinkle with green onions and peanuts.

Printed in Great Britain
by Amazon